Edwin Hall

An exposition of the law of baptism

As it regards The mode and the subjects

Edwin Hall

An exposition of the law of baptism
As it regards The mode and the subjects

ISBN/EAN: 9783337132057

Printed in Europe, USA, Canada, Australia, Japan

Cover: Foto ©Lupo / pixelio.de

More available books at **www.hansebooks.com**

AN EXPOSITION

OF THE

LAW OF BAPTISM;

AS IT REGARDS

THE MODE AND THE SUBJECTS.

BY

EDWIN HALL, D. D.

PROFESSOR OF THEOLOGY, AUBURN THEOLOGICAL SEMINARY.

PHILADELPHIA:
PRESBYTERIAN BOARD OF PUBLICATION,
1334 CHESTNUT STREET.

EDITOR'S PREFACE.

The Committee have much satisfaction in bringing within the reach of the churches a new edition of Dr. Hall's admirable work on "The Law of Baptism." Originally written for the defence of the truth in the author's congregation, and published at their desire, the work met with an unlooked for demand, and was stereotyped and widely circulated. The book being out of print, and the plates destroyed by fire (or lost), the author has presented the copyright of the work to the Presbyterian Publication Committee, by whom it has been stereotyped and issued in the present form, after revision and emendation by the author.

"The Law of Baptism" has been widely useful in the past, and is eminently adapted to meet the difficulties and doubts of inquirers, and to overthrow the prejudices and misconceptions of those in error as to the mode or subjects of Christian Baptism.

INDEX.

I. PRINCIPLES OF INTERPRETATION 7
II. SCRIPTURAL MODES OF BAPTISM 46
III. DISSERTATIONS UPON PARTICULAR POINTS, TOUCHING THE INTERPRETATION OF THE WORD BAPTIZE:
   1. Classic Greek and the Greek of the New Testament 100
   2. Mr. Judd on Mark vii. 4. 106
   3. Dr. Campbell on Mark vii. 4, and Luke xi. 38. 107
   4. Prof. Ripley on Mark vii. 4, and Luke xi. 38. 110
   5. Baptist Missionary Translations 116
   6. Scriptural Idea of Baptism 121
   7. Translating the word Baptize 126
   8. Transferring words from one language to another 132
   9. Martin Luther's Version 136
   10. The Peshito-Syriac Version 139
   11. Dutch, Danish, and Swedish Versions 142
   12. The Vulgate 144
IV. SCRIPTURAL AUTHORITY FOR INFANT BAPTISM 149
V. OBJECTIONS ANSWERED. THE UTILITY OF INFANT BAPTISM VINDICATED 199

THE LAW OF BAPTISM.

I.

MODE OF BAPTISM.

THE PRINCIPLES OF INTERPRETATION.

Go ye, therefore, and teach all nations, BAPTIZING them in the name of the Father, and of the Son, and of the Holy Ghost.—MATTHEW, xxviii. 19.

THE disciples of Christ are to be *baptized*. So all evangelical Christians agree; and such is the law of Christ. But while there is an entire agreement with regard to the *authority* of the law, there has arisen a difference of opinion concerning its *interpretation*. All the leading denominations of Protestant Christendom, save one (and it is to Protestant Christendom, if anywhere on earth, that we are to look for intelligent views of doctrine and of order, and for evangelical obedience), all the leading denominations of Protestant Christendom, save one, maintain that the *mode* of baptism is not essential; and for this opinion they go, not to the decrees of the Pope, nor to the traditions of the Papal Church, as we have been slanderously reported, but to the Word of God. Upon the most careful examination, and in making the best and most scrupulous application of the acknowledged rules of interpretation that we are able, we find that *sprinkling* and *pouring* are Scriptural modes of baptism. Many think further (and I profess myself of this number), that these are the *only* modes for which we have any clear Scriptural example, or even clear Scriptural authority, if anything is to depend upon the *mode*. But we think nothing depends on the mode:—that the command to Baptize refers to the *thing done*, rather than to the *mode* of doing it: viz., to a *ritual purifying by some manner of application of water;* and in which the *mode* of the application is a matter of entire indifference; provided it be done decently and reverently, as becomes an ordinance of God. Hence, we regard immersion as valid baptism; and never refuse to administer it in that mode, when the candidate for baptism cannot be satisfied in conscience with any other.

But while we believe these things, another large denomination of Christians deem it *essential* to baptism, that the *whole body be immersed;* and so essential, that they refuse to be united in church membership, or to partake, even occasionally, of the Lord's Supper in company with others who hold the same Gospel truth and order; who are of acknowledged piety; who, according to their best understanding, and with the full conviction of their conscience, have been baptized; who differ from themselves only in not having been wholly under water in the manner of their baptism; and who, were they to be convinced that immersion is essential to baptism, would as soon throw their bodies into the fire as refuse to be immersed. Their fault is not *wilful disobedience;* it is not *neglect;* it is not any want of *candor* or *diligence* in examining the question concerning the mode of baptism; it is solely this: instead of subjecting their judgment and conscience in this matter to the authority of their Baptist brethren, they have presumed to follow their *own* judgment and their *own* conscience, as enlightened by a careful study of the word of God.

"To the law and to the testimony." That word shall judge us in the last day, and by that will we be determined now.

In our investigation of the MODE OF BAPTISM, I shall first remark concerning *the principles of interpretation to be applied or admitted in determining this question.*

Then I shall, upon the basis of these principles, institute three inquiries:

1. What would the immediate disciples of Christ understand from the simple face of the command, "Baptize?"

2. Is there satisfactory evidence that they always

administered the ordinance of baptism by immersion?

3. On the supposition that our Lord was baptized in a given mode, and that the apostles always practiced that mode; is there evidence that they considered that one mode essential?

The preliminary remarks concerning the *principles of interpretation*, together with an *application of those principles* to the method of arguing employed by our Baptist brethren, will occupy this first discourse. I shall be obliged to take up subjects foreign from the common field of sermonizing; and such as are rather scholastic, and not very interesting to a mixed assembly. I shall be obliged to tax your patience somewhat; but I will make the matter as clear and as interesting as I can, and discuss no topic which you will not perceive to have a weighty bearing upon the argument before we get through.

There cannot be much Gospel in such a discussion as this; as the whole genius of the Gospel is averse to disputations about the *mere modes* of rites and ordinances. I will try, however, to discuss the matter in the spirit of the Gospel; and will endeavor to bring in as much of the Gospel of salvation as a disputation about the mere *ceremony* of an ordinance will admit. I proceed

1. TO THE PRINCIPLES OF INTERPRETATION TO BE APPLIED OR ADMITTED IN DETERMINING THIS CASE.

Sir William Blackstone, in his " Commentaries on

the Laws of England," cites the following example for the purpose of illustrating one of the principles on which laws are to be interpreted.*

"A law of Edward III. forbids all ecclesiastical persons to purchase *provisions* at Rome." Now the word "*provisions*" commonly means "*victuals*," "*things to eat;*" and at first sight the law of Edward III. seems to forbid the purchasing of *victuals* — meat, grain, eatables — at Rome.

Suppose now, on a debate concerning the import of this law, one should say, "The law is express: it says, 'provisions,' and provisions are 'victuals.'" Granted: such is the common acceptation of the word. Suppose he should urge it, and bring a hundred dictionaries, in all of which the first and most common meaning of the word "provisions" should be "victuals." Suppose, when I question whether the law meant victuals, and endeavor to give my reasons, he should lift up his hand toward the sun, and cry, "It is as plain as the sun in the heavens, and the man who does not see it is not worth arguing with: all the dictionaries say so: it has been conceded a thousand times that 'provisions' means 'victuals.'" Suppose he should go further: suppose he should hunt up the word "provisions" as used in all the classic English authors from the days of Chaucer and Spenser, and show in ten thousand instances that the word provisions

---

* Blackstone, Introduction. §§ 2, 3.

means victuals; and that, even in its figurative uses, it still refers to something to *support* and *nourish:* e. g. as when Mrs. Isabella Graham selected a multitude of texts of Scripture calculated to give her comfort in death, she called them "Provisions for passing over Jordan." "Here," says the stickler for victuals, "here I take my stand. If I have not settled the meaning of the word 'provisions,' nothing can be settled." And so he stretches the law to his dictionaries and classics. Provision *shall* mean victuals; and all further reasoning is barred away from any concern in settling the question.

You have here, if I mistake not, and as I think I shall be able to show, the substance of the Baptist principles of arguing concerning the question at issue.

But no, says Blackstone; see first for *what reason* the law was made. Search out the meaning of the word "provisions," with reference to what was intended to be forbidden by that law.

"The law," says Blackstone, "might seem to prohibit the buying of grain and other victuals; but when we consider that the statute was made to repress the usurpations of the Papal See, and that the *nominations to benefices by the Pope* were called *provisions,* we shall see that the restraint is intended to be laid on such *provisions* only."

The word "provisions" in this law of Edward III. does not mean grain or victuals, or stores of any kind; but "nominations to ecclesiastical benefices by

PRINCIPLES OF INTERPRETATION. 13

the Pope;" and for this law people may purchase as much meat and grain and other victuals at Rome as they please. The decision of Blackstone carries all common sense with it. Away go the hundred dictionaries and the ten thousand quotations from the classics. No matter how many times it might have been "conceded" that the word provisions commonly means something to eat. Blackstone himself makes the same concession, and still maintains his interpretation of the law.

No matter then, though a hundred dictionaries of classic Greek, and ten thousand quotations from classic Greek writers, should give *immerse* as the common and universal meaning of the word *Baptizo*. These classic Greek writers lived in another and distant country, and from three hundred to eight hundred years before Christ. They were heathen. They had never used the word with reference to a religious ritual, any more than they had used other words of their language to express the Christian ideas of Holiness, Sin, Faith, Repentance, Justification, Salvation, Angel, and Church. These words, carried into a country where the true God was known, and applied to ideas of the true religion, immediately assumed a meaning which they had never expressed in the land of classic Greek. The Greek language was not introduced into Judea till after the conquest of that country by Alexander, more than three hundred years before Christ. The Hebrew continued to be spoken with the Greek;
2

and it is even contended, with no small force of argument, that Matthew wrote his Gospel in Hebrew; as Paul (Acts xxi. 40) stood on the stairs of the castle, and spake to the people "in the *Hebrew tongue.*" When Christ came, the word *Baptizo* and rituals called "Baptisms" had been in common and every day use among the Jews for about three hundred years. Thus (Heb. ix. 10) the Jewish ritual service is said to have "stood only in meats and drinks, and *divers washings.*"—(διαφόροις Βαπτισμοις— *divers baptisms.*) Mark vii. 4. speaks of the (Βαπτισμοὺς ποτηρίων, καὶ ξεστῶν, καὶ χαλκίων, καὶ κλινῶν) "baptisms of cups and pots, brazen vessels, and of tables" (or of couches). The same passage says of the Jews, that when they come from the market, (ἀπο αγορᾶς— from places of public concourse,) "except they *baptize themselves,* (μὴ Βαπτισωνται,) they eat not." Accordingly, (Luke xi. 38,) when Jesus sat down to meat in the Pharisee's house, the Pharisee marvelled "that he had not first washed before dinner," —(ὅτι οὐ πρῶτον εβαπτισθη—that he *had not first been baptized* before dinner.) The custom of baptizing themselves was so common as to make it a matter of wonder that Jesus should once sit down to dinner without being baptized. We have only to ascertain what that custom was, to ascertain what they understood by the word baptize. We cannot settle that question by any amount of quotations from classic Greek writers. We must allow Matthew, and Mark, and Luke, and Paul, to testify concerning the use of the word in their country and their day, and by themselves, just as we must allow the heathen Greeks to testify concerning its meaning when used by themselves. Where the New Testament use differs from that of the classic Greek, it is to be adopted as the true one, so far as this question is concerned, even though the heathen Greeks should be unanimous and uniform in giving another meaning to the word, in their country and in their day. The word is so common in the New Testament and in the Septuagint; it is used with reference to rituals, whose mode is so well defined as to render its meaning absolutely certain: and I think I shall be able to show with absolute certainty that that meaning is not truly given by the word *immerse*. It is altogether idle — and I think I shall be able to show that it leads to utter error and falsehood — for one to pretend to "fix the meaning of the word" from the classic Greek, and to determine beforehand, on such a basis, that the New Testament writers *must* use the word in that sense. The Bible is God's own word, and surely the Holy Ghost must be a competent and credible witness, with regard to the meaning with which the Holy Ghost uses the word *baptize*.

Let me give an illustration or two of the effect of arguing the New Testament meaning from the original and from the classic use of a word.

Some years since I met with a man who was liberally educated, a thorough scholar, an able lawyer, and possessed of splendid natural abilities, but skeptical in his views of religion.

With this man I undertook to reason of the necessity of being born of the Holy Ghost. Now, the word in the Greek Testament for Ghost, or spirit, is *Pneuma* (πνευμα), which originally, and in the classic Greek, most commonly meant WIND. This man would have me argue by book. He turned me to the Greek Testament (John iii. 5). "See here," says he, "it reads, and you know it reads, 'Verily, verily, I say unto thee, except a man be born of *water* and of WIND, he cannot enter into the kingdom of God.' What right," said he, "have you to change the original classic meaning of '*Pneuma*' (πνευμα), '*wind*,' here, any more than you have of '*Hudatos*' (ύδατος), '*water?*' And see further," said he, "there is the same word in the 8th verse — letter for letter — and there you do not say, the '*Spirit* bloweth where it listeth;' you say, 'the WIND bloweth where it listeth.'

He was right in the original and ordinary classic use of the word. And if I had argued on the principles on which (I shall show) our Baptist brethren have argued, I should have been obliged to allow, that the renewing by the "Spirit of God," or even the personal existence of such a Spirit, is not taught or referred to in this passage.

With all due respect for our Baptist brethren, I humbly conceive that, in this matter, they have fallen into an egregious error in their attempted corrections of our common translation.

To the Bibles and Testaments issued by their society, they prefix a glossary, containing, among others, the following words, thus:

"*Meaning of the words used in this translation.*"

Αγγελος,	Angel,	Messenger.
Βαπτιζω,	Baptize,	Immerse.
Βαπτισμος,	Baptism,	Immersion.
Εκκλησια,	Church,	Congregation."

It is maintained that these words, and some others, are improperly, if not dishonestly, left untranslated in the received English version, and that the words which are given in the third column ought to be substituted for the words adopted in our translation. Thus: where we read "Church," we ought to read "Congregation;" where we read "Angel" in our version, we ought to read "Messenger;" where we read "Baptize," we ought to read "Immerse;" and where we read "Baptism," we ought to read "Immersion."

Now it appears to me that this is falling into a worse error than that of the unbelieving scholar concerning the word *Pneuma*, or Spirit. Thus, "Angel" is a word of Greek original adopted into the English language, and used in our translation.*

---

* Nothing is more common than such adoption of words from the Greek. The process is going on to this day; particularly our terms of science and of art are almost wholly adopted (and compounded) from the Greek. Strike all such

Our Baptist brethren insist that this adoption is wrong: that the word ought to be translated by the word "Messenger."

It is certainly true that, in the classic Greek, the word ANGEL (αγγελος) means *Messenger;* and means nothing like the idea which we attribute to it: viz., of a spiritual being of an order superior to man and inferior to God. The Greeks even had another word to signify such a spiritual being, "*Demon*" (δαιμων), and *Angelos* (αγγελος) meant nothing but "*messenger.*" But mark how the classic Greek was modified when adapted to Jewish ideas. The Jews used the word "*Demon*" (δαιμων) to express only an *evil* spirit; a *fallen* angel; and "*angel*" they appropriated to the *good* spirits. And to translate the word in all cases as the Baptist Bible Society would teach us, instead of adopting it into English, would make the most arrant nonsense.

For example: take Acts xxiii. 8, and translate it according to the instructions and on the principles of the Baptist Bible Society.

In our common version the passage reads thus:

---

adopted words from our language, and scarcely could two people, even in the ordinary walks of life, hold a conversation for a single hour.

"Et nova *fictaque nuper* habebunt verba fidem si
GRÆCO *fonte* cadant, PARCE DETORTA."

"Licuit SEMPERQUE LICEBIT
Signatum præsente nota producere nomen."
Q. HORAT. *Ars Poetica.*

PRINCIPLES OF INTERPRETATION.   19

"For the Sadducees say there is no resurrection, neither angel nor spirit: but the Pharisees confess both." The word *resurrection* here falls under the same rule, if you take its meaning from the classic Greek. The Greeks had no such idea as that of the resurrection of the body; and of course no word for it, but their αναστασις (*anastasis*) was a simple "rising up." In our translation the passage reads thus: "For the Sadducees say there is no *resurrection*, neither *angel* nor *spirit;* but the Pharisees confess both." According to the principles on which our translation is branded as inadequate and unfaithful, we must read it thus: For the Sadducees say there is no *rising up*, neither MESSENGER nor WIND." But did they ever say so? Did they ever deny the existence of such a thing as a messenger, or of such a thing as wind?

According to the glossary prefixed to the Bible by the Baptist Bible Society, we must expunge the word *angel* from our Bibles, and substitute the word *messenger*. Thus, John v. 4, must be read, "For a *messenger* went down at a certain season into the pool, and troubled the water." In Acts xi. 13, we must read, "And showed us how he had seen a *messenger* in his house:" Acts xii. 15, "Then said they, it is his" (Peter's) *messenger:*" Matt. iv. 11, "Then the devil leaveth him, and behold *messengers* came and ministered to him:" Matt. xviii. 10, "Their *messengers* do always behold the face of my Father in Heaven:" 1 Cor. vi. 3, "Know ye not, that we shall judge *messengers?*" Heb. i. 4, "Being made so much better than the *messengers;*" Heb. ii. 16, "He took not on him the nature of *messengers;*" and Heb. xiii. 2, "For some have entertained *messengers* unawares." I confess that there is quite as good reason for making Angel read messenger, as there is for making Baptize read immerse."

The word *Church*, too, must express no more than the heathen idea of a town-meeting, or assembly. But clearly the New Testament *ecclesia* does mean something which it never could mean in classic Greek. Thus, in 1 Cor. xii. 28, "And God hath set some in the *Church*, first Apostles," &c.; it is not a simple *assembly*, or *congregation*, that is intended; so, Eph. i. 22, "And gave him to be head over all things to the *Church*," it is no congregation that is intended, but the universal policy of Christ's people, in all lands, at all time, on earth and in Heaven. Perhaps we should not have had either *Church* or *Angel* proscribed from the Bible, had it not been essential to find some company for the poor banished word Baptize.

The same reason existed for converting the Greek *Baptizo* into the English *Baptize*, as for converting *Angelos* into *Angel*. There was no word in English which would fill up the idea. If baptism was to be performed by sprinkling, it would not do to translate *Baptizo* by the word sprinkle, because all sprinkling is not baptism. If baptism were exclusively by immersion, still the word immerse would not express the whole or the essential idea; and all immersion is not baptism. The word *Baptize* in the New Testament refers less to the manner of the application of water, than to the *design* and *import* of the application; it is a sacred application: a ritual application: denoting a ritual purifying, and referring to an important and essential truth for its signification. The New Testament use of the word involved a reference to these ideas, just as the word *Baptize* does now; and neither of the words, *sprinkle, pour, immerse*, has the essential quality of referring to these ideas. Thus: if I go and throw myself off from one of the wharves at high tide, I am immersed beyond question; but am I baptized? Our young men and boys immerse themselves many times every summer; but are they baptized? I think all would deem it improper to say so. The fundamental idea of baptism is wanting.

It would therefore be an inadequate and improper translation to substitute the word *immerse* for the word *baptize*, in every place in the New Testament; as much as it would to make that substitution which should make the Sadducees deny the existence of such a thing as a "messenger," or "wind." The translators of our Bible, as intelligent and honest men, *could* not translate "*Baptizo*" by "*Immerse*" on this ground alone: and I shall show that they could not on another: as in the New Testament the word denotes often an application of water (or of something else), by *sprinkling* or by *pouring*. It is used often where the idea of immersion is entirely excluded.

Indeed, if any fault is to be found with the word *Baptize*, as though it were a Greek word, instead of a translation, precisely the same objection applies to the words "*Immerse*" and "*Immersion*." These are as purely Latin, as "Baptize" is Greek: and we might with the same propriety turn round and say, Why do you not translate those Latin words? Do you mean to "keep people in ignorance," and "promote a union of Church and State," by talking to the people, like the Pope, in Latin?

To my mind, the noise that is made about the non-translation of the word Baptizo, is utterly without foundation. To adopt the principles on which the noise is made, and carry them out, would lead to gross absurdity. To say that people would never have made any question about the *mode* of baptism if the word had only been translated *immerse*, is only to say that if the word had been improperly translated, the people would have been misled. There is no reason in the world, that I know of, for thinking that our translators were either ignorant or dishonest in this matter. Had they not turned *Baptizo* into an English word, they must have expressed it by a circumlocution that would have amounted to a gloss, rather than a translation, or they must have coined a new word for the purpose.

Besides, while so large a part of the learned world fully believe that Baptism in the New Testament often signified an application of water which was performed by sprinkling or by pouring; how could we have a Bible in which all denominations may agree, if we insist upon translating the word Baptize either by "*immerse*," by "*pour*," or by "*sprinkle?*" Were there no other reason, this would be sufficient for adopting the original word, instead of translating it by either.

And yet, our Baptist brethren have broken off from the national Bible Society, for the very reason that it will not be thus instrumental in putting forth to the world a sectarian Bible! They have a denominational Bible Society, entitled the "*American and Foreign Bible Society*," which issues its foreign translations on the principle of substituting the word immerse for baptize: and by their notes at the beginning of the New Testament they have, in effect, done the same for the English translation: with how little reason, I have shown.

I say not this out of disrespect or fault-finding. The right of conscience and of private judgment is theirs. Most freely, with no disturbance or complaint on our part, let them enjoy it. I only aim to point out what I consider the error of the principle. Whether I have succeeded, you will judge. We impeach not their integrity in the least. Would that *our* integrity in this matter, and *our* rights of conscience and of private judgment, might be equally respected. But it is with no less grief than astonishment, that I read in the papers the last month, the following "*Resolution*" of the "American and

Foreign Bible Society," at their anniversary on the 28th of April of the present year.*

"*Resolved*, that by the fact, that the nations of the earth must now look to the BAPTIST DENOMINATION ALONE FOR FAITHFUL TRANSLATIONS OF THE WORD OF GOD, a responsibility is imposed upon them, demanding for its full discharge, an unwonted degree of union, of devotion, and of strenuous and persevering effort throughout the entire body."

That our Baptist brethren mean to be faithful in translating the word of God, we doubt not. But are we to believe that all the missionaries of Protestant Christendom throughout the world, save "the Baptist denomination alone," have given to the poor heathen *unfaithful* translations of the word of God? Can no "faithful translation" come from any denomination on earth save one?† Are the "nations

---

* A.D. 1840. It was moved by Prof. Eaton, of Hamilton Institute, and seconded by Rev. Mr. Malcom.

† In the report of the American and Foreign Bible Society, for 1840 (p. 89), the translations made by all other denominations are stigmatized as "Versions in which the real meanings of . . . words, are PURPOSELY KEPT OUT OF SIGHT," . . . so that "Baptists cannot circulate *faithful* versions . . . unless they print them at their own expense." They ask (p. 40), "Shall we look on unconcernedly while unfaithful versions (as we hold them) are circulated?" They assert (p. 45), "It is known that the British and Foreign Bible Society, and the American Bible Society, have virtually COMBINED TO OBSCURE at least a part of Divine Revelation;" and

of the earth," according to the tenor of this resolution, dependent on "the Baptist denomination alone" for this?

that "these societies . . . continue to circulate versions of the Bible, unfaithful, at least so far as the subject of baptism is concerned; and that they are by this means propagating their peculiar sentiments under the auspices, and at the expense of the millions of all denominations who contribute to their funds; and who are thus made the unconscious instruments of *diffusing the opinions of a party, instead of the uncorrupted word of Jehovah.*"

This last paragraph is not less remarkable for its deliberate charge of dishonesty upon all other denominations than for its singular admission of that, which if it be a fact—it seems to me—is fatal to the immersion scheme. The allegation is, that to transfer *baptizo* into BAPTIZE, instead of rendering it by the word *Immerse,* is "*to propagate the peculiar sentiments*" of Pedobaptists. That is, the word *baptizo* is so used in the New Testament, as almost without fail to lead those who learn its meaning from the Bible alone to conclude that it does not, in the Bible, mean immersion; and if you leave people to learn its meaning from the context for themselves, you "propagate the peculiar sentiments" of Pedobaptists among them! Nay, the same effect will be produced when such a Bible is given by Baptist hands, and accompanied by Baptist instructions! If Baptists circulate such a version, they "are thus made the unconscious instruments of *diffusing the opinions*" of the "*party*"—of Pedobaptists!

I believe it. It is even so. But the conclusion is (and the objection of our Baptist brethren unwittingly adopts this very conclusion as its basis), that the word *baptizo,* as it is used in the New Testament, does not mean immerse; and

Having remarked so far upon the principles of interpretation, I come now to make an application of those principles to the mode of arguing adopted by our Baptist brethren.

It was first attempted to prove that *Baptize* means exclusively to immerse, from the *etymology* of the word. *Baptize* is truly a derivative from *Bapto:* and the primitive meaning of Bapto is to "dip," or to "immerse." It was contended that it *always* means to immerse. This was long urged and most strenuously insisted on as the foundation of the Baptist argument—that *Bapto* means nothing but to dip or immerse.

But upon examination it was found that the meaning of *Bapto* had undergone important changes; that it often meant only to *color*, from an allusion simply to the known EFFECT of dipping, and not to the ACT of dipping: and so it is often used, in instances where dipping is wholly out of the question. Thus Hippocrates says of a certain liquid, that when it *drops* upon the garments, they are "*Bapto'd*," or *stained*. They are *Bapto'd*, by DROPPING *the liquid upon* them.*

---

will not be so understood by those who judge of its meaning by its *use* in the sacred writings. But to insinuate that Pedobaptists mean to "corrupt the word of Jehovah," or "to diffuse the opinions of a party," instead of the "uncorrupted" word of God, by so transferring the word, can scarcely be believed.

* Carson, p. 60.

So Homer, speaking of a battle of frogs and mice on the borders of the lake, says (ἐβάπτετο αἵματι λίμνη)—"The lake was *Bapto'd* with blood." In order to maintain the position that *Bapto* always means *immerse*, it was contended that, by a figure, the lake was here represented as *dipped* in the blood of a mouse! Indeed, on the ground then taken by Dr. Gale and by others, it was necessary to contend for this; for if they could not make it out, their foundation was gone. But since Carson showed the absurdity of the ground, it has been generally abandoned. And yet, while the ground is given up, the tracts based on this ground are still in circulation, and do their work in making proselytes on the strength of an argument which well-informed Baptists have in general given up as thoroughly exploded. Such a change in the meaning of a word is a very common occurrence, and it is conceded on all hands that the *derivation* of a word is no certain index to its meaning.

Thus the word " *Tint* " comes from a Latin word (Tingo), which originally meant to *dip*, then it meant to *color* or " *tinge*," and now we speak of the " *tints* " of the clouds or of the flowers, without ever thinking that the flowers or the clouds have been *dipped* to give them their coloring. So the word "*Spirit*" comes from the Latin "*Spiritus*," of which the original meaning was "*a breath*." But what mortal will now contend that a spirit is nothing but breath?

And yet there is the same reason for complaining that the word *spirit* is an untranslated Latin word, that there is for complaining that *Baptize* is an untranslated Greek word, and the reason from etymology for making *spirit* mean breath is just as strong as for making *Baptize* mean immerse from its derivation from Bapto. So the words "*bind*" and "*bonds*" originally meant to tie up or manacle with cords or chains. But who thinks now of putting cords or fetters on a man when he is "*bound*" to keep the peace or to appear in court, or when he is put under "*bonds*" to fulfil the condition of a bargain or agreement?

The mode of making out immersion from the derivation of Baptizo having been overthrown, and its very elements scattered to the wind, the learned Carson has taken another ground, and this is the one now universally relied on. I refer to Carson, because his research has made this field his own on the Baptist side of the question, because he is undoubtedly a very learned and able man, the chief, indeed, on the Baptist side in this part of the field of controversy, because their writers are fond of referring to his arguments as something which can never be overthrown, and because, indeed, all the more recent works, to which I have had access, are little else than Carson over again. For these reasons I shall follow his argument, fully confident that if it does not stand in him, it will never stand in the strength of any man.

Mr. Carson has with immense labor hunted over the Greek classics, and found, as he thinks, that the word Baptizo always means, in classic Greek, to dip or immerse. That this is its common meaning in *classic* Greek is certain, though I think he has failed to make it out to be its exclusive meaning.

Having settled its classic meaning, he then attempts to make the New Testament meaning in every instance conform to it. Here lies the tug. He cannot accomplish this unless we will allow him to take for granted the thing to be proved. The New Testament use is — as I think I shall show — most clearly and indefeasibly against him.

Here lies his error, and it is fundamental. He relies on the classic Greek to determine the New Testament Greek, while the facts in the case are as much at war with his conclusions, as the facts in another case would be with the conclusions which should interpret "provisions" in the law of Edward III. to mean victuals, or with the reasonings which would make our Lord say, that men must be born of "water and of wind," or with those which would make the Sadducees deny that there is any "messenger" or "wind."

Here is a point to be settled. What do Matthew, and Mark, and Luke, and John, and Paul mean by *Baptize?* To settle this point Homer, and Pindar, and Xenophon are brought up to testify as to the meaning of the word in their country and in their day. Does this settle the question? Is it certain that the word, when adapted to *Jewish* ideas and *Jewish* rites, meant precisely what it did in the days of Homer and Pindar? I humbly conceive it might be as well to call the Evangelists and Apostles themselves, and ask *them* what they meant. But, says the examiner, Pindar, and Homer, and the rest of the Greek classics, have settled the question what Evangelists and Apostles must mean, and so, I shall show, he determines that they shall mean, if he has to get this meaning out of them by torture. But what is the use of calling up Matthew, and Mark, and the Apostles, as witnesses at all, if the question is settled before they come?

Carson, having finished his appeal to the classics, takes his position. He takes his "position" before we are through with the evidence, or even come to that part of the evidence on which the question really turns. Before coming to the New Testament he says (p. 79), "*My position is, that it always signifies to dip, never expressing anything but mode.*" He admits that he has all the lexicographers against him,* and I shall show that if the lexicographers

---

* Our Baptist brethren have the lexicographers against them on the question of the *exclusive* sense *immerse* more thoroughly than many of them seem to be aware of. All the lexicographers give other significations. And even the learned Cox is much mistaken here. He defies us (p. 83) "to point to a single lexicon which does not give *dipping, plunging,* or *immersing,* as the unquestionably settled, and universally primitive meaning of the word."

make any account of the New Testament or of the Christian fathers, they ought to be against him. His

---

The defiance can be met, and that on authority which our Baptist brethren are fond of quoting as the very best — the *native Greek*. *Mr. R. Robinson* (Hist. of Bapt.), quoted in Pengilly (p. 72), says [and it is often fondly repeated], "The native Greeks must understand their own language better than foreigners, and they have ALWAYS understood the word *baptism* to signify *dipping*." "In this case, the Greeks ARE UNEXCEPTIONABLE GUIDES." If our Baptist brethren choose to make an issue here, be it so. Simply to meet this challenge, I copy the following from Chapin's "Primitive Church," pp. 43, 44.

"The oldest native Greek lexicographer is HESYCHIUS, who lived in the fourth century of the Christian era. He gives only the word Βαπτω [*bapto*], and the only meaning he gives the word is αντλεω [*antleo*], to *draw* or *pump* water.

"Next in order comes SUIDAS, a native Greek, who wrote in the tenth century. He gives only the derivative Βαπτιζω [*baptizo*], and defines it by πλυεω [*pluno*], *to wash*." — "We come down to the present century, at the beginning of which we find GASES, a learned Greek, who, with great labor and pains, compiled a large and valuable lexicon of the ancient Greek language. His book, in three volumes quarto, is a work deservedly held in high estimation by all, and is GENERALLY USED BY NATIVE GREEKS." The following are his definitions of *bapto* and *baptizo*. (Ed. Venice, 3 vols., 4to,)

"ΒΑΠΤΩ [*bapto*].
  —Βρεχω [brecho], *to wet, moisten, bedew*.
  —πλυνω [pluno], *to wash* [*viz. clothes*].
  —γεμιζω [gemizo], *to fill*.
  —Βυθιζω [buthizo], *to dip*.
  —αντλεω [antleo], *to draw, to pump water*.

mistake lies here: he has appealed to Pindar, and Aristotle, and the rest of the heathen classics, while the proper appeal lies not TO these, but FROM these to Paul, and Matthew, and Mark, and Luke, and John, and the fathers who wrote in Greek. He has taken his stand too soon, and decided the question before coming to the most important testimony.

But having made his appeal and taken his position, Paul and Mark must be stretched on his bed of heathen classics; and I shall show how unmercifully they are stretched and racked in the process.

Thus, when in the Apocryphal book of Ecclesiasticus, which was translated into Greek for the use of the Alexandrian Jews, about 170 years before Christ, it is said (Eccl. xxxiv. 30), "He that *washeth*

ΒΑΠΤΙΖΩ [*baptizo*].
—Βρεχω [brecho], *to wet, moisten, bedew.*
—λουω [louo], *to wash, to bathe.*
—αντλεω [antleo], *to draw, to pump water.*"

The work is principally a translation of Schneider's Greek-German Lexicon, upon which Passow's is based. The significations constitute rather a glossary than the strict definitions of a lexicon, and each signification is applicable, not to every passage in the language, but only to its own class of passages.

Though this is sufficient evidence that the word, among the Greeks, does not exclusively mean *to immerse*, we base no argument on the credit of any lexicographer. The sole object of making this reference is to meet the confident challenge which is so constantly thrown out by our Baptist brethren.

himself because of a dead body and toucheth it again, what availeth his *washing.*" The word *washeth* here is Βαπτιζομενος — "BEING BAPTIZED." The allusion is to Numb. xix. 16.

"And whosoever toucheth one that is slain with a sword in the open fields, or a dead body," &c. — "A clean person shall take the hyssop, and dip it in the water, and *sprinkle* it upon the tent," &c. . . . "and upon him that toucheth a bone, or one slain, or a grave." The conclusion should be, I think, inevitably, that the baptizing here was done by sprinkling, and that here is a clear instance in the Alexandrine Greek in which the word baptize is used to denote a purification by sprinkling, with no reference to dipping or immersing at all.

But Carson says, No. "When I have proved the meaning of a word by the authority of the whole consent of Greek literature, I will not surrender it to the supposition of the strict adherence of the Jewish nation, in the time of writing the Apocrypha, to the Mosaic ritual."

The question then comes to this dilemma; either the Jews had *abandoned* this mode of purifying from a dead body, as specifically and minutely pointed out by God — or, *here was* A BAPTISM BY SPRINKLING. Carson is driven here to *assume*, and that without the least shadow or pretence of authority, that when God had commanded a purification by sprinkling, the Jewish nation had turned about and made an immersion of it. If we do not allow this assumption to pass with no proof, and receive it as an established certainty, then Carson's "position" has been overthrown, and here is a *baptism by sprinkling*.

But difficulties multiply upon him as he proceeds. Thus, in Mark vii. 4: "And when they come from the market, except they *wash*, they eat not." The original is, "Except they *baptize themselves*, they eat not;" which, I shall show hereafter, is, Except they "*wash their hands*," *i. e.*, perform a ceremonial purification upon them.

The learned Campbell, who wished very much to establish immersion as the proper meaning of baptism, could see no other mode of getting along here than by supposing that their hands were dipped, and so the immersion (or baptism) predicated of the hands. He knew very well that no history of Jewish customs could furnish a scrap of evidence to show that whenever Jews had been in the market, they always immersed their whole bodies. But unfortunately for him the original language is so definite as to show conclusively that the baptism here spoken of is the baptism of the *persons:* "Except *they* (the persons) are baptized;" not "Except their *hands* are baptized." Carson reproves this fault of Campbell (p. 101), and says, that Dr. Campbell's notion that this baptism refers to the hands as a washing by "dipping them" he "does not approve." He very properly calls it "an ingenious conceit, without any authority from the practice of the language." But how does Carson himself dispose of the difficulty? In a very summary way, indeed. He has shown the meaning of *baptizo* from the heathen classics; and he proves the universal custom of the Jews, always to *immerse* themselves, from the meaning of the word! I beg his pardon; the meaning of the word is the very thing that is in question here. We cannot allow him to prove a matter in question by first assuming it as true. What is the *historical fact* as to what the Jews did before eating whenever they came from the market? Settle this, and you settle the meaning of the word baptize in this connection. But no; Carson is determined that the historical fact shall be settled by the meaning of the word, and the thing in dispute shall be proved by itself; no matter though all history is against it. He has proved the meaning of the word from the heathen classics; and no matter for any difficulties in the way; the Evangelist *shall* mean immersion by it. No matter though it is proved that the Jews purified themselves by pouring water on the hands; and that "the manner of the purifying of the Jews" was from "water pots, holding about three firkins" (at the largest computation about two-thirds of a barrel) "a-piece," from which water might be *poured*, or *run* on the hands; but in which no man could be immersed. "I care not," says he, "that ten thousand such examples were brought forward;" he insists that the word *baptize* shall here mean to *dip*, viz., to dip the whole body;

"because Greek literature so uses the word baptize." No matter how improbable it may be that the Jews always immersed their whole bodies as often as they came from the market; no matter though no record or trace of such a custom is found anywhere in the world, unless it be in this assumed meaning of the word baptize; no matter though no such custom has been heard of the Jews, wherever they have been dispersed throughout the world for so many ages to this day; no matter that though the purifying is still kept, it is still performed by pouring water on the hands, or holding them in a stream of water running from a vessel,—Carson maintains still and stoutly that, "We have here the authority of the Holy Spirit for the Jewish custom." "If," says he, "I have established the acceptation of this word by the consent of use, even an inexplicable difficulty in this case would not affect the certainty of my conclusion." I humbly beg leave to differ from him; and you may judge whether I have alleged sufficient reason. The Holy Spirit has indeed said that the Jews were *baptized* as often as they came from the market; but the Holy Spirit has not said that the word baptize here means to immerse. The *meaning* is the thing *in question*. And it seems to me, that a reference to the plain facts in the case authorizes us to consider rather this, that the Holy Spirit regarded that as a baptism of the person, which was performed by pouring water on the hands, as I shall show more particularly hereafter. If Carson has failed here, he is overthrown, and entirely so. I do think that he is shown to have reasoned from false principles, and to have failed. And I know of few among the more intelligent Baptists, who will not be ready to admit, that if the very basis of Carson's argument be overthrown, the whole fabric of their peculiar system is broken up and falls to the ground.

Carson argues in the same manner with regard to baptism of the tables (couches) in Mark vii. 4. He says (p. 114), "But with respect to Mark vii. 4, though it were proved that the couches could not be immersed, I would not yield an inch of the ground I have occupied." Now how shall we argue with a man who will not admit an absolute impossibility to be any obstacle in the way of his theory; the couches were baptized, and if it "be proved" that "the couches could not be immersed," he will not yield an inch; he will maintain still that they were *immersed.* "And I may add," says he (p. 116), "that the couches might have been so constructed, that they might be conveniently taken to pieces." Indeed! what shall we not allow him to suppose might have been, rather than grant the possibility that the Jews "*might*" have used this word "baptize" in a sense different from that of the old heathen Greeks?

Nor would it seem to make any matter to Mr. Carson, how often people had been "baptized" in other modes than immersion; he would still maintain his ground. "I care not," says he, "I care not if there had never been a human being immersed in water since the creation of the world, if the word denotes immersion, and if Christ enjoins it, I will contend for it as confidently as if all nations had been in the practice of baptizing" (immersing) "each other" (p. 155). True, IF the word means *immerse*, and NEVER means anything else. But I humbly suppose that the common practice of a people who called a purifying by sprinkling or pouring, a *baptism*, would have some little weight upon the question what that people did in fact understand by the words "baptize" and "baptism."

So when Carson comes to the baptism of the Holy Ghost, it is nothing to him that the Scriptures represent this uniformly under the mode of "pouring," "coming down like rain," and "shedding forth." He says, "It is a fixed point, that baptism means immersion;" "and in the examination of the reference in the baptism of the Spirit, NOTHING CAN BE ADMITTED inconsistent with this;" and then adds (p. 164), "The baptism of the Spirit must have a reference to immersion, because—*baptism is immersion!*" I would reply, *That*, Mr. Carson, is the very thing to be proved; whether baptism is, exclusively, immersion. But he insists upon it directly in the same page, and puts his words in italics— "*Pouring cannot be the figurative baptism, because baptism never literally denotes pouring.*" "*Pouring* could not represent the pouring of the Spirit, because the Spirit is not literally poured."

I would reply, — But, Mr. Carson, does not God himself say, "I will *pour* out my Spirit?" But, replies he, "Believers are said to be *immersed into* the Spirit, not because there is anything like immersion in the manner of the reception of the Spirit, but from the resemblance between an object *soaked* in a fluid, and the sanctification of all the members of the body and faculties of the soul" (pp. 167, 168).

I say nothing about the resemblance between "soaking" and "sanctifying," but he says truly, there is "nothing like immersion" in the manner of receiving the Spirit, nor, of course, is there in the manner of conferring it; yet a *baptism* there is, Christ being witness, and the *mode* of that baptism is represented by a "*pouring out*," "*shedding forth*," "*coming down*," "*falling upon*."

But immediately Mr. Carson responds (p. 168), "There was a *real* baptism (immersion) in the *emblems* of the Spirit."

I answer, Christ did not say, ye shall be "immersed" into the "emblems" of the Spirit; he said, "ye shall be *baptized* with the HOLY GHOST," with the Spirit itself, not with its "emblems."

I would follow Mr. Carson further here, did I deem it necessary. But I think I have gone far enough to show that he has failed, most signally failed, in that which is the very foundation and element of his argument. He will prove everything if we will let him assume everything. But we cannot. His principles of reasoning are unsound, and if you allow him these unsound principles, he still begs the question. You have seen how the Evangelists are put to the torture when they are stretched on this Procrustean bed of the heathen Greeks. Even granting that Carson has rightly settled the question with regard to the heathen Greeks, I think I have shown his argument to be as inconclusive as that which should make the word "Provisions" in the statute of Edward III. mean *victuals*, or as that which would make regeneration consist in being born of "water and of wind," or as that which would make the peculiar infidelity of the Sadducees consist in denying that there is any "*rising up*," or "*messenger*," or "*wind*."

We might rest the debate here, but I think that Carson has even failed to make out his case from the Greek classics. The limits of this work forbid me to enter upon an extended survey of this part of the field; nor is it necessary, as a failure in a single instance is fatal to Mr. Carson's argument. Take, then, the instance cited by Mr. Carson (p. 61 of his last edition)—the Sybilline verse quoted by Plutarch in his life of Theseus—which, says Mr. Carson, "exactly determines the meaning of baptizo." Theseus consulted the Oracle at Delphi concerning his government. The Oracle predicted the safety of the new state, and identifying Theseus with his state, it concluded with the words, "Thou shalt ride a bladder in the surge;" or in the free translation of Langhorne:

"Safe o'er the surges of the foaming tide."

With this, says Plutarch, agrees the Sybil's prophecy concerning Athens, Ἀσκὸς Βαπτίζῃ δῦναι δε τοι οὐ θέμις ἐστιν. To this verse Mr. Carson gives the following translation:

"Thou mayest be dipped, O bladder, but art not fated to sink!"

I agree with Mr. Carson that this exactly determines the meaning of the word Baptize in this connection, and is worth a hundred ordinary passages for fixing critically the accurate classical meaning; but unfortunately for Carson's argument, it fixes it against him.

The ασκος (*askos*) is the ancient bottle, of the whole skin of an animal, which, blown up like a bladder, rides the waves without sinking or even suffering an immersion. The Oracle says, "Thou mayest be *baptized*, O bottle, but it is not allowed thee to—δῦναι (*dunai*). Determine the meaning of *dunai* here, and you fix the meaning of *baptize* in the same connection. Mr. Carson assumes that it means to *sink*, in distinction from a simple dipping into or under. But such is not its meaning. Whoever will consult the numerous instances cited by Donnegan will perceive that the primary meaning of the word is as he states it, "*to go into or under,*" "*to enter,*" "*to penetrate.*" This primary idea is the one which he clearly traces in all the examples of its secondary signification. Not an example can be found in which it signifies to sink, in distinction from a simple dipping. The idea is that of *entering, penetrating* (by passing from one medium into another), e. g. Βελος εις εγκεφαλον δῦ, the arrow penetrated the brain. Hom. II. xviii, 376.

So Crusius, in his Homeric Lexicon (translated by Prof. Henry Smith), gives, as the primary signification of the word, "*to go into, to enter, to penetrate into, to plunge into,*" which primary senses he traces in all the instances of its secondary significations throughout the Homeric writings. Nowhere does it signify a *sinking*, in distinction from a simple *immersion*, as Mr. Carson erroneously supposes. It is used for entering into a house, into a city, into a cave, and for plunging into the SEA, where it certainly signifies no sinking, in opposition to a simple immersing.

The meaning is so certain that the derivative δυτης signifies a *diver;* certainly not one who sinks, rather than one who simply plunges in and rises again. So the other derivative δυτικος signifies one expert in diving; surely not one expert in sinking to his destruction, and that in direct opposition to simply plunging in and coming up again. The meaning of δυναι is further corroborated, and rendered absolutely certain, by the consideration that when a sinking is to be signified, or any thorough *going down*, κατα δυω (the intensive compound of δύω) is employed.

The Oracular line then reads thus:
"Thou mayest be *baptized*, O bottle, but it is not allowed to thee to *go under.*" Thou mayest be *dashed, wet, washed,* but it is not possible for thee to *penetrate, go under.* Here is a classic baptism in which it is impossible for the subject to go under water.

Take another of Mr. Carson's examples, p. 58. "Plutarch, speaking of a Roman general dying of his wounds, says, that having *dipped* (*baptized*) his hand in blood, he wrote the inscription for a trophy." "Here," says Carson, "the mode of the action cannot be questioned. The instrument of writing is dipped in the coloring fluid." Suppose we grant it. My *pen* is the instrument of writing, and I *dip* it in the ink when I write; surely I *never immerse* it in ink when I write. When will our Baptist brethren cease this play upon the word *dipping*, when they are to prove a total immersion!

Another instance is cited by Carson (p. 21) from Aristotle, of "a land uninhabited, whose coast was full of sea-weeds," which at ebb tide, μη αττιζεσθα', was not baptized, but at full tide, καταχλυζεσθαι, was dashed over by the waves. The opposite of not being baptized here is, not the dipping of the land in the waves, but dashing the waves over the land, or, if you please, washing over it, overflowing it. Mr. Carson even is compelled to admit that "the water comes over the land," and that "there is no actual exemplification of the mode expressed by this word" (viz. in his sense of immersion). Yet very preposterously, as it seems to me, he still contends that the word here "still expresses that mode," and strange! that "the word has been employed for the very purpose of expressing it" (viz. the mode of *immersion* in this application of water to the land)!

Take another example (Carson, p. 59): Homer representing the death of one of his heroes, says, "He struck him across the neck with his heavy sword, and the whole sword became warm with blood." On this one scholiast remarks, that "the sword is represented as *baptized* in blood." Another says, "In that phrase Homer expresses himself with the greatest energy, signifying that the sword was so *baptized* as to be even warmed" (ὡς βαπτισθεντος ὐντω του ξιφους, ὡς τε θερμανθῇναι); "by a strong figure," says Dr. Pond, "it might be said to be *bathed* in blood. But in this case the bathing must have been effected by the blood flowing over the sword." And Prof. Ripley says at last, "the sword was so *overflowed* [with blood] as even to become heated."

So where Aristophanes, in his account of the Platonic banquet (Ripley, p. 17), says, "I am one of those (βεβαπτισμενων, baptized) *drenched* yesterday," viz. with wine. He had not been *immersed* in wine, even in figure. So in another place, one had *baptized* (βαπτισασα) Alexander with wine. The figure is of drenching, not of immersing.

Mr. Carson's ancient classics fail him, and we have seen that if they did not, their entire agreement, in using the word to denote only an immersion, would by no means settle the question. We must go to the New Testament. We must learn the sacred use of the term. We must learn what Evangelists and Apostles deemed essential to baptism, and if we make anything essential which they did not, we are found guilty of adding to the word of God.

II.

MODE OF BAPTISM.

SPRINKLING AND POURING, SCRIPTURAL MODES.

So far, we have been occupied in discussing the principles of interpretation to be applied or admitted in determining what it is to baptize; and in making an application of these principles to the mode of argumentation adopted by our Baptist brethren.

I now proceed to the three inquiries laid down as the plan of my argument in the preceding chapter.

I. WHAT WOULD THE IMMEDIATE DISCIPLES OF OUR LORD UNDERSTAND FROM THE SIMPLE FACE OF THE COMMAND "BAPTIZE?"

II. IS THERE SATISFACTORY EVIDENCE THAT THEY ALWAYS ADMINISTERED THE ORDINANCE OF IMMERSION?

III. ON THE SUPPOSITION THAT THEY DID SO, IS THERE EVIDENCE THAT THEY CONSIDERED THAT ONE MODE ESSENTIAL?

I. *What would the immediate disciples of Christ understand from the simple face of the command* "BAPTIZE?"

In Heb. ix. 10, we read of a ritual service, "which stood only in meats and drinks, and divers WASH-

INGS." In the original, it is (διαφοροις βαπτισμοις), "DIVERS BAPTISMS."

There were, then, under the Old Testament dispensation, rituals, which, for three hundred years (or from the time that the Greek language was introduced into Palestine), were commonly called *baptisms*. We have only to learn what these rituals were, to determine the meaning of the word *baptize* in the common language of the country in the time of Christ. The apostle does not leave us in doubt of this; for he proceeds immediately to specify one of these baptisms, in v. 13, as "the blood of bulls and of goats, and the ashes of a heifer *sprinkling* the unclean." If these sanctify "to the *purifying* of the *flesh*, how much more shall the blood of Christ *purge your conscience!*"

The persons and things were never immersed in blood; they were *sprinkled;* and these sprinklings Paul here calls *baptisms*. It should be noticed, too, that as the *sprinkling* of the ashes of a heifer, sanctifieth to the purifying of the "flesh," so the application of the "blood of Christ," which purgeth "the conscience," is repeatedly called the "SPRINKLING" (never the immersion) "of the blood of Christ."

The "PURIFYING OF THE FLESH" by the ashes of a heifer, to which Paul here refers, is prescribed in Numbers xix. 17, 18. "And for an unclean person, they shall take of the ashes of the burnt heifer of purification for sin, and running water shall be put thereto in a vessel, and a clean person shall SPRINKLE it upon the tent, and upon all the vessels, and upon the persons that were there, and upon him that touched a bone, or one slain, or one dead, or a grave."

It is added, that on the seventh day "he shall bathe himself;" and our Baptist brethren are fond of saying that the "Baptism refers to the bathing." I am glad of the objection, because it distinctly recognizes the fact that Paul refers to these purifyings as among his "DIVERS BAPTISMS." But the objection is idle, as Paul does not specify the "*bathing*" as any part of what he means; but he does specify the "*sprinkling*." He does not say that the bathing* "sanctifieth to the purifying of the flesh," but he says it is "the blood of bulls and goats, and the

---

* If he did, the word *bathing* would not necessarily imply an immersion. *Bathing* here is synonymous with *washing*.

Dr. Edward Beecher remarks, that " of *persons*, no immersions at all are enjoined under the Mosaic ritual." "No washing of persons is ever enjoined" by the word *tabal*, to immerse, even in a single instance, nor by any word that denotes immersion—but, as I think, without exception, by the word *Rahhats*, which denotes to *wash*, without any reference to mode." "Those who read the English version might suppose that, where the direction to bathe occurs, immersion is enjoined; but in every such case the original is only to wash." The word used in the command, is the same as that used in Gen. xviii. 4, "Let a little water, I pray you, be fetched, and *wash* your feet." Gen. xliii. 31, "And he *washed* his face, and went out." So Levit. xiv. 9. "Also, he shall *wash* his flesh in water, and he shall be clean."

ashes of the heifer SPRINKLING the unclean, that sanctifieth." It is what is done by another hand (for a "clean person" must sprinkle the unclean), on which Paul's mind fastens as the baptism; and he does not deem it necessary to specify anything else. And this application of blood, which was made by sprinkling, and the ashes of a heifer sprinkling the unclean, Paul calls a baptism.

The current of his discourse leads him on to speak of another of the "divers baptisms," in ver. 15, and onward. Having made a comparison between the "purifying of the flesh" by the sprinkling of blood, and of the ashes of a heifer, and the "purging of the conscience" by the "sprinkling of the blood of Christ," he runs out the same parallel between the ritual of establishing the first testament under Moses, and the ritual of establishing the second under Christ. It is worthy of remark that the same form of ritual is still kept up; it is still a sprinkling, and not an immersion. "For when Moses had spoken every precept to all the people, according to the law, he took of the blood of calves and of goats, with water, and scarlet wood, and hyssop, and *sprinkled* the book and all the people. Moreover, he *sprinkled* likewise with blood both the tabernacle and all the vessels of the ministry." The argument is, that Christ, in ratifying the new covenant, must ratify it with his own blood; and the only modal application of this blood spoken of even in figure, is the "*sprinkling* of the blood of Christ." The current of his discourse, and the contrast which runs throughout his argument, shows that the "divers baptisms" are still referred to in these purifyings so repeatedly described under the mode of *sprinkling.*"

He speaks of "*divers baptisms.*" Another of these is mentioned in Numb. viii. 7: "And this shalt thou do unto them to cleanse them" (viz. the Levites, to prepare them to enter upon the functions of their office), "*sprinkle* water of purifying upon them, and let them shave all their flesh, and let them wash their clothes, and so make themselves clean." Note here, that no man inducts himself into the priesthood, and all that was done to the Levite by *another's* hand was the "*sprinkling.*" The leper was in like manner to be cleansed by sprinkling, Lev. xiv. 9. And so pre-eminently is the sprinkling considered as the important element in the cleansing, that this alone is the outward part of the ritual pitched upon to designate the purifying with which Christ washes away the sins, and cleanses away the pollution of the soul. Thus, Isaiah lii. 15, "So shall he sprinkle many nations." Heb. xii. 24, "And sprinkling of the blood of Christ." 1 Pet. i. 2, "And sprinkling of the blood of Christ." You never read of his "*Immersing* many nations," nor of the "*Immersion* of the blood of Christ;" no, never, in the word of God.

But the IMPORT of baptism by water is this same cleansing away of sin by the blood of Christ. The washing away of sin is effected—not by the water—

but by the blood of Christ. Baptism by water signifies this washing away of sins. Thus, "Arise, and be baptized, *and wash away thy sins.*"* Now if the application of the sign is to resemble the application of the thing which performs the real cleansing, and to resemble it even in figure; if the type is to resemble the antitype; the shadow the substance; then as it is the sprinkling of the blood of Christ that DOES the cleansing, surely it should be the *sprinkling* of the water in baptism that SIGNIFIES the cleansing; immersion would spoil the resemblance, and mar the significance of the sign.

But not to come at the conclusion too soon, let us hold here upon the testimony of the facts so far considered. We have here, then, "DIVERS BAPTISMS" performed by SPRINKLING.

Turn now to Mark vii. 3, 4—" For the Pharisees, and all the Jews, except they wash their hands oft, eat not; holding the tradition of the elders. And when they come from the market,† except they

---

* There is a curious mode of setting aside this argument, by considering baptism as designed to represent the burial and resurrection of Christ! The word of God gives quite another view of the import of baptism; see Acts ii. 38, and xxii. 16.

† Rosenmuller says, " The sense is, 'when they come from the market (*i. e.* any public place), they do not take their food except they wash their hands.' Αγορα (the market) signifies not only a concourse of men, or place of public

wash, they eat not; and many other things there be which they have received to hold, as the washing of cups, and pots, and brazen vessels and tables."

The words *"wash,"* and *"washing"* are in the original (βαπτισωνται), except they HAVE BAPTIZED THEMSELVES; and (βαπτισμους), "BAPTISMS."

See how this subject is introduced. "And when they saw some of his disciples eat bread with defiled (that is to say, with unwashen) hands, they found fault." Then follows the explanation: "For the Pharisees, and all the Jews, except they wash their hands oft, eat not; and when they come from the market, except they wash, they eat not." See Matt. xv. 2—"Then the Pharisees and Scribes asked him, Why walk not thy disciples according to the tradition of the elders,* but eat bread with unwashen hands?" Compare this with Luke xi. 38. A Pharisee marvelled that the Lord Jesus "had not first *washed* before dinner" (original, εβαπτισθη); that "he had not first BEEN BAPTIZED before dinner." The

---

resort, in which provisions are sold, and in which trials are held, but all similar public places. Αγορα—public places, opposed to private dwellings.

* " The rule of the rabbins was, that if they washed their hands well in the morning the first thing they did, it would serve for all day, provided they kept alone; but if they went into company, they must not, at their return, either eat or pray, till they had washed their hands "—*Matthew Henry*, on Mark vii. 4.

fault of the Lord Jesus and of the disciples, in the eyes of the Jews, was, that they had not first been BAPTIZED (or *baptized themselves*) before eating; *i. e.*, they had eaten with UNWASHEN HANDS. The washing of the hands, therefore, was a *baptism;* and, as the form of the original language, as well as our translation, shows, a baptism of the persons, not simply of the hands, *i. e.*, they (the persons) were baptized when their hands had been washed for a ceremonial purifying.

There is this further peculiarity about it; their hands were not commonly *dipped* or *immersed*, but washed in *running* water, as streaming from a pitcher or from a watering pot.*

---

* The practice is continued in the Eastern world to this day. Before meals, a servant comes round with a pitcher, and *pours* water on the hands of those about to eat, or they are otherwise cleansed with *running* or *streaming* water. The custom is a very old one, as is apparent from 2 Kings, iii. 11, "Here is Elisha, the son of Shaphat, who *poured water* on the hands of Elijah," *i. e.*, who was *servant* to him: the very common *duty* of a servant is used as an appellation to designate the *relation* of a servant.

The custom of washing the hands before eating, as it still prevails in the East, was this: "When they wash, the water is poured from a vase upon the hands over a basin—they never make use of a basin or a tub to wash in, as is the practice elsewhere."—*Oscanyan in Kurtz*, p. 179.

In John ii. 6, &c., where there were set six water-pots of stone, after the manner of the purifying of the Jews; at the time of the middle of the feast these water-pots appear to

I am aware that attempts have been made to set aside the force of these passages, in Mark vii. and Luke xi. But these attempts have done no more than to demonstrate the strength of our position. There are only two possible grounds of resisting the conclusion. One of which is, that the baptism is predicated of the *hands*, as though the hands were immersed; and the other, that while the Jews on many occasions WASHED *their hands*, yet as often as they *came from the market*, they IMMERSED their whole bodies.

As was noticed in the previous discourse, Dr. Campbell takes the first ground, and Mr. Carson the second. Campbell, appearing to know full well the absurdity of supposing that "all the Jews" always "immersed" themselves as often as they came from the market before eating, referred the baptism to the hands, and maintained an immersion, but an immersion of the hands only. Carson replies, that he considers Campbell's view of the matter as "nothing but an ingenious device, without any authority from the practice of the language." Such it most undoubtedly is. No scholar could ever have been be-

---

have been *empty*. The purifying (which Mark and Luke call a baptizing) had been performed, not by the guests immersing themselves or dipping their hands in the water-pots, but by "drawing out," and probably by carrying and pouring the water on the hands. If this be so, then our Baptist brethren are left destitute of that last, but unavailing refuge, the "dipping of the hands."

trayed into such a "device," save from the hard necessity of making out an "immersion" in this case, by some means or other. Carson, on the other hand, maintains that we are taught here, that "all the Jews," whenever they have been at the market, never eat *except they have immersed the whole body.* He says (p. 68), " It ought to have been translated 'except they dip themselves they eat not.'" What does he bring to prove it? The word *baptize;* baptize means immerse; therefore they were immersed, the Holy Spirit being witness! But the very question is, *whether* baptized means immerse. The Holy Spirit has said they were baptized, and has so explained it as to leave us to understand that they were baptized (ceremonially purified) by washing their hands. The Holy Spirit has said they were baptized, but the Spirit has not told us that by *baptize* he means *immerse.*

What was the fact? Did the Jews always immerse themselves as often as they came from the market? To me it appears clear that the Holy Spirit has explained what the fact was; they washed their hands. And what does Mr. Carson bring to show that they always immersed their whole bodies as often as they came from the market? Nothing but this idle begging of the question concerning the word baptize. There is not a scrap of evidence in anything else in the wide world to show it. The manners and customs of the Jews were well known. They have been known since throughout the four quarters of the globe, wherever their nation has been scattered and peeled; the washing of the hands still exists; but nothing—no, nothing from all history has been adduced to show that they observe, or ever observed the custom which Mr. Carson here attributes to them. Nothing—no, nothing, but this idle begging of the question has been alleged and substantiated, or can be. But all this matters nothing to Mr. Carson! High, low, rich, poor; at home and abroad; winter or summer; all are conveniently furnished with baths, or with something else, where they may conveniently immerse themselves before eating, as often as they have been at the market! It matters nothing that these things were never heard of; "baptize means immerse," and therefore it must be so. It matters not, that "according to the manner of the purifying of the Jews," there were set, not "*baths*," but "*water-pots;*" and that those used at the marriage supper in Cana, when they would seem to need "much water" if ever, contained about "two or three firkins a-piece" (somewhat over half a barrel, according to the largest computation, large enough, it would seem, to purify a whole company of guests, but of questionable capacity for a single immersion. No; no matter for difficulties. "No," says Carson, "even an inexplicable difficulty would not affect the certainty of my conclusions." But enough; I think you will conclude with me, that here is sufficient proof, that Mark, speaking as he was moved by the

Holy Ghost, teaches us that the word "baptism" was used to denote (among other things) a *ritual washing of the hands.* Of course, the immersion of the whole body is in no way essential to a baptism.

The mutual contradictions of our Baptist brethren, in the evasions which they attempt on this passage in Mark vii. 3, 4, only show the absolute certainty that baptism here means no immersion. While Carson says, p. 307, " Either the persons referred to were immersed, or the inspired writer testifies a falsehood," Mr. Woolsey says, p. 158, " There is not sufficient ground for believing that the Jews immersed their whole body when returning from the market." With him agrees Professor Ripley, who says, " In the absence of clear satisfying proof, it is not becoming to make positive assertions." Baptist writers generally maintain that, on the occasion referred to, they only immersed their hands. But the sacred record says, " Except *they* (βαττισωνται) baptize *themselves!*" it mentions no *part* of the body, but refers the baptism to the person, as absolutely as in any case whatever. To insert the word hands here is to alter the diction, and pervert the meaning of the Holy Ghost. And so Carson argues; for, p. 68, he says, " When no part is mentioned or excepted, the whole body is always meant."

Baptist writers generally maintain that, on the special occasion of coming from the market (αγορας), they perform an *immersion;* (some say, an immersion of themselves; others, an immersion of their hands; and others, an immersion of their victuals; while on other occasions they simply *wash* their hands. The very connection of the passage refutes this distinction. Where had Jesus and his disciples been, when the Jews complained that his disciples eat with unwashen hands? Turn to the verse preceding this seventh chapter, and you will see. They had been in the "villages," "city," "country," and "*streets.*" But the word "*streets*" is in the original αγοραις (*agorais*), precisely the word rendered in vii. 4, *market*. Jesus and his disciples then had come from the markets; and the Pharisees wondered that they eat bread with defiled (that is to say with *unwashen*) hands. Then follows the explanation: and it is making no tautology to understand the last clause as a specific example (applicable to the case in hand), of the general custom mentioned in the first; "For the Pharisees, and all the Jews, except they wash their hands oft, eat not," (here is the general custom, they wash their hands "oft;" then follows the particular instance, applicable to the case in hand); "And when they come from the *market*, except they wash (baptize themselves), they eat not." They had just come from the market-places (αγοραις); and the wonder was that they did not baptize themselves: that is, that they eat bread with unwashen hands. Such is the explanation which the Scripture gives of the sense in which the Scripture uses the word "baptize"

This view is still further corroborated by the passage in Luke xi. 38: Jesus had been working miracles, and engaged in giving continued instructions. Nothing was said to show that it was in a market; though, attracted by his instructions, a crowd had gathered round him. "And as he spake, a certain Pharisee besought him to dine with him; and he went in and sat down to meat. And when the Pharisee saw it, he marvelled that he had not washed before dinner" (in the original $ἐβαπτίσθη$, that he had not been baptized). Did the Pharisee wonder that Jesus had not immersed his whole body, before eating an ordinary meal? Did the Pharisee immerse himself? Did he offer to lead Jesus to a bath? Was there any retiring and unrobing for an immersion? Or must we not suppose, rather, that the Pharisee washed his own hands on the spot, from the use of some "water-pot," "after the manner of the purifying of the Jews;" and wondered that Jesus (as had been complained of his disciples) eat with "unwashen hands?"*

Here the word of God says that the Pharisee

---

* Nor is the common evasion of our Baptist brethren, concerning dipping the hands, possible here. The word *ebaptisthe* is in the passive voice, and does not admit the word hands to be understood as its object. Nor are we allowed to supply it by synecdoche; for where an author omits so to limit his meaning to a part, we have no authority to alter his meaning by supplying it. The word "hands" is not in this passage, or near it. The sacred writer refers absolutely to the baptism of the person.

wondered because Jesus once sat down to meat without first having been baptized. Was the custom of immersing the whole body so universal before eating dinner, as to make it a matter of wonder that Jesus should once omit it? There was no such custom. "The manner of the purifying of the Jews," on such occasions, was by pouring water on the hands; and the persons were then said to be baptized. The word *hands* is not in this passage, but the wonder was that he (Jesus) had not first *been baptized* (ὅτι οὐκ πρωτον ἐβαπτισθη). The person then was baptized by *pouring water on the hands*. Such is the testimony of the word of God, as to the meaning of the word common in that country at that day.

One thing further is to be observed here. The word *washed* (*ebaptisthe*), in Luke xi. 38, is, letter for letter, in all respects precisely the same as that used in Mark i. 9, "Jesus" (*ebaptisthe*) "was baptized of John in Jordan." In Luke xi. 38, the Holy Ghost affirms the baptism of the person as fully, as absolutely, as unequivocally, as he does when he says Jesus was baptized of John in Jordan. Yet the baptism in Luke xi. 36, was no immersion, but a simple ablution of the hands, by pouring, or allowing water to run over them. Nay, the Holy Ghost uses in this case the selfsame word, without the alteration of a single letter, without a syllable of explanation, with no circumstance to modify or diminish the full meaning of the word baptize. How then can it be pretended from the meaning of the word alone, that Jesus was *immersed* of John in Jordan? Why could not the baptism in this case be performed by *pouring* water on him, as well as in the other? With this explicit and unequivocal testimony of the Holy Ghost, as to the common meaning of "baptize" in the sacred writings, how can our Baptist brethren pretend, that when our Saviour commands us to be baptized, he commands us to be immersed, without being guilty of altering the command of Christ, and adding to the word of God?

To my mind, here is, so far, demonstration—proof which puts it beyond my power to doubt—that *sprinkling* and *pouring* are SCRIPTURAL MODES OF BAPTISM. Whether the mode of immersion has a scriptural recognition is a matter that is yet to appear. It is certain, without going farther, that IMMERSION CANNOT BE ESSENTIAL TO BAPTISM.

Let us come now to the use of the word "baptize" with reference to the work of the Holy Spirit. Jesus said, Acts i. 3, "John truly baptized with water, but ye shall be baptized with the Holy Ghost, not many days hence." I will not stop to show how grossly this would sound to alter it, according to the proposal of our Baptist brethren, so as to read, "But ye shall be immersed with (or in) the Holy Ghost."

This baptism was accomplished on the day of Pentecost. Peter said of it, "This is that which was spoken by the prophet Joel: And it shall come to pass in the last days—I will *pour out* my spirit *upon* all flesh." "He (Jesus) hath *shed forth* this." So, Acts xi. 15, 16, "And as I began to speak, the Holy Ghost *fell* on them, as *on us* at the beginning. Then remembered I the word of the Lord, how that he said, John indeed baptized with water, but ye shall be baptized with the Holy Ghost." The mode of the baptism here spoken of, is under the figure of pouring and shedding forth. The gift of the Spirit is never spoken of under the figure of immersion, but as a pouring, shedding forth, sprinkling, coming down like rain. Thus, Isaiah xliv. 3, "I will *pour out* my Spirit upon thy seed." Ezek. xxxvi. 25, 26, "Then will I *sprinkle* clean water upon you, and ye shall be clean: a new heart also will I give you." Compare Tit. iii. 5, 6, "By the washing of regeneration, the renewing of the Holy Ghost, which is *shed on us* abundantly;" Ps. xlii. 6, "He shall come down upon the mown grass as *showers* that water the earth;" Isaiah lii. 15, "So shall he *sprinkle* many nations."

It has been argued that the baptizing was still by immersion, as the Spirit was shed down "abundantly," and "filled the room." The Scripture says, "the sound" filled the room. It is not so gross as to speak of the Holy Spirit filling a room like a material substance, and thus immersing people. Besides, though you might cover people by pouring water on them, provided they were enclosed in a room or vessel, you could not be said to "dip" or "plunge" them in so doing; but immersion (and it is contended that the baptism of the Holy Ghost shall be called the "immersion" of the Holy Ghost), has the act of dipping entering necessarily into its idea, as well as the act of covering. Moreover, all converted persons are *baptized* with the Holy Ghost. Paul says, 1 Cor. xii. 13, "For by one spirit are we all baptized into one body, whether we be Jew or Gentile, bond or free." But who will pretend that all converted persons are "immersed" into the Holy Ghost, according to the manner in which (it is argued) the apostles were immersed on the day of Pentecost, by pouring the Spirit upon them till it filled the room, and so immersed them?

Here I rest under this topic. The *mode* of baptism in the baptism of the Holy Ghost, as that mode is indicated by the uniform figure, is *pouring, shedding forth, sprinkling,* coming down like rain, or like *showers, falling upon.* I cannot but wonder that those who insist so much upon the words, "buried with him in baptism," are not able to see in these also an equal authority for proper modes of baptism; even granting (what I do not grant) that their favorite phrase has some reference to a *mode* of baptism.

Having traced the meaning of the word "baptize" so far in the Scriptures, turn to the EARLY CHRISTIAN FATHERS, whose views of what is essential to baptism were moulded on the meaning of the term common among Christians and Jews. The following examples, with several others, are adduced by Dr. Pond.*

"TERTULLIAN speaks of baptism being administered by sprinkling. 'Who will accommodate you, a man so little to be trusted (asperginem unam aquæ) with one *sprinkling of water?*'

"ORIGEN represents the wood on the altar, over which water was *poured* at the command of Elijah (1 Kings xviii. 33), as having been baptized.

"LACTANIUS says that Christ received baptism, 'that he might save the Gentiles by baptism,' that is (purifici roris perfusione) by the *distilling of the purifying dew.*

"CYPRIAN, JEROME, and some others of the Fathers, understood the prediction, 'I will *sprinkle* clean water upon you,' Ezek. xxxvi. 25, as having reference to water baptism.

"CLEMENS ALEXANDRINUS, speaking of a backslider, whom John was the means of reclaiming, says, 'He was baptized a second time *with tears.*'

"ATHANASIUS reckons up eight several 'baptisms,' and the sixth in his enumeration is that "*of tears.*'

GREGORY NAZIANZEN says, 'I know of a fourth baptism, that by martyrdom and *blood;* and I know of a fifth, that of *tears.*' The baptism of tears and

---

* See pp. 33, 34, of his excellent work on Baptism.

blood was a favorite phraseology with the early Christians."

Now in all these baptisms, of the "wood and the altar," of "tears," and "blood," the idea of "dipping," "plunging," "burying," or "immersing," is excluded. "Wet," "washed," "sprinkled," "poured upon," those spoken of here as baptized might be; but whether men may be dipped or immersed in their own tears or blood, admits of a question. If it be said that these representations are figurative, certainly there is no immersion about them, even in figure.

The conclusion is, that the early fathers, as well as the Apostles, understood the word "baptize" in quite another sense than that of immerse. Their idea of baptism was that of a *purifying* (or consecrating) by *sprinkling* or *pouring*, and these are the modes under which is constantly represented the purifying (the baptism) of the Holy Ghost.

I have now done with the argument under the first head, and we are ready for the question, *What would the immediate disciples of our Lord understand from the simple face of the command* "BAPTIZE?" Would they consider *immersion* as ESSENTIAL? I think the conclusion is inevitable; IT IS IMPOSSIBLE. Sprinkling and pouring they would inevitably consider lawful and proper modes; and so far, it has not appeared that they have any notion of immersing at all; or any authority for it, if direct authority be sought for a specific mode.

6*

I have done with the argument from the meaning of the word, and proceed to the second inquiry.

II. IS THERE SATISFACTORY EVIDENCE THAT THE DISCIPLES OF CHRIST ALWAYS ADMINISTERED BAPTISM BY IMMERSION?

I say *always;* for if they did not always do so, immersion cannot be essential, even though it could be proved (which it cannot be) that immersion was the common mode.

John was baptizing in Enon, *"because there was much water there."* It is contended that the "much water" could be needed only for immersion, and that therefore John baptized by immersion.

It is not a little remarkable that they who print this in capitals to prove that John baptized by immersion, presently find water enough in Jerusalem to baptize three thousand in a small part of one day. They are fond of asking, "WHY DID HE GO TO THE RIVER?" They dwell much upon "FOLLOWING THE SAVIOUR DOWN THE BANKS OF JORDAN;" and upon "GOING TO THE RIVER." But though Jordan was at hand, we read no more about the disciples going "to the river." We hear nothing said by the Apostles about following the Saviour down the banks of Jordan. They baptize wherever they may happen to be; and are never at a loss, or compelled to remove to another place for the purpose of finding "much water." It does not appear that they ever think it needs much water for baptism. It seems strange, therefore, that John went to Enon to find much water for the mere purpose of baptizing.

John preached "in the wilderness" (Matt. iii.) it is said, Mark i. 4, "John did baptize in the wilderness." It is said that "Jerusalem and all Judea, and all the region round about, went out to John." Such multitudes would need "much water" for other purposes than immersion; and John must needs resort to a place where much water might be found to furnish those multitudes in the wilderness with drink, unless indeed he could work a miracle, and we read that "John did no miracle." This may seem, at first view, a little matter to us, in this land of wells, and brooks, and springs; but all who are familiar with travels in the East, know how important a considerable caravan finds it to get near a good watering place for an encampment, even for a single night.

Now what was this "Wilderness of Judea?" Take the map and look eastward from Jerusalem and Judea to Jordan, to the region lying between these, and from the Dead Sea up to what is supposed to be Enon. You have embraced the location of the wilderness of Judea. And what is this wilderness? An American lady (Mrs. Haight), who travelled up this region from Jericho a short time since, thus describes her journey in Vol. ii. p. 131, of her travels. "Our course lay due north, up the valley of Jordan. We *replenished our water-bottles* (bags), as we were warned that we should find no more until afternoon.

At this spot we left all signs of cultivation; the plain was afterward *one entire desert,* during the whole day's ride of twenty-five miles. The soil was a compact gravel, or as geologists call it, a 'hard pan,' partially covered with a short dry grass, the result of the winter rains, which withers up the moment their influence is past. Not a single object or incident occurred during this most tedious and painful day of all my life. This was the first time since we left Beyroot that we had suffered any length of time for want of water. By nine o'clock the intense heat of the sun made the water in the leather bottles so warm that we could not drink it. Extreme thirst obliged us merely to moisten our parched tongues."

Josephus bears the same testimony of this wilderness. "The whole plain," says he, "is destitute of water, except the Jordan." In another place he says, that "The Jordan, dividing the lake of Gennesareth in the midst, passes through an extensive desert into the Dead Sea."

In this wilderness John was preaching and baptizing. There seems here reason enough why, being in the wilderness, he should *"go to the river,"* even if it were not to immerse; and reason enough why he should resort to Enon for much water, even for other purposes than immersion. The immense multitudes would need water for drink; or if they had prudently brought a supply in their leathern bags, John might still have preferred the waters of the river for the purpose of purifying; and the traveller,

Sandys,* says, "that at Enon are little springs gushing out, whose waters are soon absorbed by the sands." Could not these springs, with their streams, have been the (πολλα ιδατα), "many waters," for the sake of which John resorted to Enon; for it cannot be supposed but that there was as *"much water"* anywhere along the stream of Jordan as opposite to Enon; and to find much water *in Jordan* could be no reason for going to *Enon* more than for "going to the river," at any other spot? We read no more of "going to the river," or of going to any spot to find much water for the *purpose of baptizing.* I leave it, therefore, for you to judge, whether the argument for immersion from going "to the river," and from going to Enon, because there was "much water there," does not dissipate and scatter away like the mists before the sun and wind.

"But Jesus *came up straightway out of the water.*"

The argument drawn from this is distinct from that of going to the river, and from the "much water" at Enon. It therefore merits a distinct examination.

Did Jesus *emerge from beneath* the surface of the water; or did he simply *go* up out of the water, or *from* the water? The original language here is such as can have no reference to emerging from under water, the Greek is αναβαινων απο του υδατος,— "*going up out of (or from) the water.*" The verb

---

* Hamilton on Baptism, p. 92.

and the preposition both forbid the idea of emerging from under water. To express this both should have been changed, and the Greek is supplied with words to express the idea exactly. And Carson, who is a profound Greek scholar, and never admits against his scheme anything that he is not compelled to admit, says (p. 200), "I admit the proper translation of απο (apo), is *from*, not *out of*. I perfectly agree with Mr. Ewing that απο (the word here translated 'out of') would have its meaning fully verified, if they had *only gone down* TO THE EDGE *of the water.*" But, says he, "My argument is this. If baptism had not been by immersion, there can be no adequate cause alleged for going to the river. Can sober judgment, can candor suppose, that if a handful of water would have sufficed for baptism, they would have gone to the river?"

I trust I have your judgment decisively given on the subject of "going to the river;" and the other part, that of "coming out of the water," Mr. Carson has formally given up. So in neither case is there the shadow of a proof, or of a presumption, that the baptism was performed by immersion. Going *into the water* (even if we admit that the Saviour went further than "the edge of the water"), and coming up *out of* the water, does not necessarily imply that one has been *under* water, or that he has been knee-deep. How much less can a simple going up *from* the water, when it is not certain that one has been *into* the water at all, necessarily imply that he had been *under* water? How idle to rely upon this to prove it?

Take now the baptism of the eunuch, Acts viii. 38, 39. "And they went down both into the water, both Philip and the eunuch, and he baptized them. And when they were come up out of the water, the Spirit of the Lord caught away Philip."

On this, Mr. Carson says (p. 203), "The man who can read it, and not see immersion in it, must have in his mind something unfavorable to the investigation of truth. As long as I fear God, I cannot, for all the kingdoms of the world, resist the evidence of this single document. Nay, had I no conscience, I could not, as a scholar, attempt to expel immersion from this account. All the ingenuity of all the critics in Europe cannot expel immersion from this account. Amidst the most violent perversion that it can sustain on the rack, it will still cry out *immersion*, IMMERSION." The fact, that in a work in which he goes over the whole field of debate, and discusses the meaning of "baptize" from old Homer to the end of Greek; the fact that in such a work, consisting of 274 pages, on the mode of baptism, he spends 24 pages upon this single passage of Philip and the eunuch, shows of how much importance he makes it; and, indeed, we are ready to suspect, from his spending so much labor on so very plain a case, that he found it not very easy to make a clear immersion out of it after all.

I profess I see no immersion in the account.

Whence is the immersion inferred? From the fact that the eunuch went into the water, and came up out of the water? But they went down *"both"* into the water, and *"they"* (both) came up out of the water. If going into the water, and coming up out of the water, prove an immersion, it proves that Philip was immersed as well as the eunuch: and what thus proves too much (proves what is not true) proves nothing.

Is it proved from the fact that the eunuch was *baptized?* What that baptizing was, is the question. I have proved that people and things were often baptized when they were not immersed, but only sprinkled or poured upon. The baptism proves no immersion.

Precisely the same words might have been used in the narrative, had they come to a stream not ankle-deep, and gone down both into* the water; and if Philip, having no convenient basin or dish, had

---

* It is not certain that they went further than *to* the water. To make the Greek εις necessarily mean *into*, would make Jesus come *into* Jerusalem, when he was as far off as "Bethphage and the Mount of Olives," Matt. xxi. 1. It would made our Lord command Peter go *into* the sea, when he was only to go *to* the sea, Matt. xvii. 27, and Peter must needs have thrown *himself into* the sea after the fish, instead of casting his hook in. These are but specimens of numerous similar absurdities.

In John xx. 4, 5, "One came (εις το μνημειον) *to* the sepulchre," "yet went he not *in*" (ού μεντοι εισηλθεν).

dipped his hand in the water, and poured or sprinkled it upon the eunuch; and if then they had both come up out of the water. Who will prove to me that this stream was a foot deep? Who will prove it a stream at all? Who will prove the quantity of water there was sufficient to render an immersion possible? If it was, who will prove that the eunuch was immersed? I see no proof of immersion here. The only show of proof is by begging the question, and taking for granted the very thing to be proved.

On the other hand there is some reason (aside from the fact that baptism was commonly performed by sprinkling or pouring), to suppose that the eunuch was baptized by sprinkling. He was reading the passage in Isaiah liii. 7, which he did not understand. Philip began "at the beginning"—viz., at the beginning of that prophecy concerning Christ (for the book was not divided into chapters and verses), and that was at chap. lii. 13—"Behold my servant." Beginning here, Philip expounded the Scripture. He must needs have read and expounded those remarkable words in ver. 15, "*So shall he* SPRINKLE *many nations.*" How sprinkle? By purifying: an inward purifying by his Spirit; and a purifying by his blood; by the "*sprinkling* of the blood of Christ;" and by the *Baptism* of the Holy Ghost. The outward sign of these inward and spiritual things is the outward purification by sprinkling. Now the explanation of this passage would most naturally lead to the conversation about baptism: the outward baptism by water. Baptism is the only ritual application of water under the Christian dispensation; and the only figure chosen to represent the spiritual cleansing by Christ is *sprinkling.* This is the only use of water foretold by the prophets, even in figure. Is it improbable that the exposition of this passage led to the conversation about baptism? And when they casually came to water, the eunuch said, "See, here is water; what doth hinder me to be baptized?" In the absence of all proof to the contrary, this incident goes to render it probable that the eunuch was baptized by sprinkling. The other instances, yet to be adduced from the sacred record, in which the baptism must apparently have been performed in some other mode than that of immersion, concur to strengthen this probability.

Two other expressions are much relied on as proof of the mode of baptism: those in Rom. vi. 3, 4, and Col. ii. 12. In these believers are said to be baptized into the "death" of Jesus Christ; and "*buried with him by baptism* into death." The language is figurative. There is just as much reason to argue from them that believers are literally put to death in baptism, as that they are literally buried under water in baptism; nay, the dying is the thing more insisted on, and, indeed, the principal idea: the one on which the whole force of the passage turns They are buried with him by baptism "into death." They are "planted together, in the likeness" (not of his grave or burial), but in the likeness *of his death*. They are "*crucified* with him." They are "baptized"—not into his grave or burial, but "into his *death*." If we are to infer the *mode* of baptism from these figures, the evidence is strongest for drawing a resemblance for the mode of baptism from hanging on the cross; for that was the *mode* of his dying; and the passage says we are "crucified with him." But the reference here is not to the mode, though the words furnish a happy sound for our Baptist brethren to play upon. The argument is, We are *dead* with Christ, and we must no more live to sin than a dead body must live. We are dead; and more—we are buried; as we often say to express strongly the fact that a person has ceased from living, "He is dead and buried." The burying is the conclusive token of his being dead: so the baptism is a token, not of the burying, but of the death; we are buried "into death;" we are baptized into his death." It is not the mode of the baptism that is referred to, but the import of the baptism:— "Our old man is crucified with him, that the body of sin might be destroyed;" "that henceforth we should not serve sin;" "that henceforth we should be *dead* to sin." I confess I see no manner of force in the argument drawn from the passage in favor of immersion. The argument being from the import of baptism rather than from its mode, both the language and the argument are equally appropriate, whatever the mode.

In 1 Cor. x. 2, the apostle says, "The Israelites were all baptized unto Moses in the cloud and in the sea." Apparently, from the quantity of water in the vicinity, this passage, as well as that in 1 Peter iii. 21, concerning the "eight souls saved by water; the like figure whereunto even baptism doth now save us,"—has been claimed as proving immersion. Surely there was water enough in the Red Sea to immerse the Israelites; and water enough in the Deluge to immerse the world, and literally to "bury it into death." But it seems to be forgotten that the "eight souls saved by water" were *in the ark*, and neither drowned nor immersed at all :* and that the Israelites who were baptized unto Moses *walked on dry land*. They suffered no immersion, unless one may be immersed on dry land. If they were wet at all, it was by the spray of the sea, and by the rain that dropped from the clouds: as in Ps. lxxvii.,

---

* To this Mr. Carson replies, p. 413, "What could be a more expressive burial in water than to be in the ark when it was floating? As well might it be said that a person is not buried in the earth, when lying in his coffin, covered with earth. May not persons in a ship be said figuratively to be buried in the sea? They who were in the ark were deeply immersed. 'Moses,' Mr. H. tells us, 'walked on dry ground.' Yes, and he got a dry dip. And could not a person, literally covered with oil cloth, get a dry immersion in the water?"

I confess I have not "perspicacity" enough to see the force of such reasoning.

"Thou leddest thy people like a flock by the hand of Moses and Aaron:" "The waters saw thee, O God: the waters saw thee; they were afraid: the depths also were troubled: the clouds poured out water." If there is any mode of baptism here, it is a sprinkling, or such a pouring out of water as falls in drops. A baptism there was; an immersion there was not.

The instances so far considered are the ones relied on to prove that immersion was the mode of baptism, and the only one practiced by the immediate disciples of Christ. I think I have shown that they prove no such thing: that they afford scarcely the faintest shadow of it; but that, on the contrary, the probability is all in favor of a baptism by pouring or sprinkling.

In the remaining instances the advocates of immersion are compelled to take the laboring oar, and render that certain or probable, which on the face of it seems impossible.

On the day of Pentecost ("the feast of weeks, of the first fruits of wheat harvest," Exod. xxxiv. 22), the season when the brook Kedron was dry, and when, "save the pool of Siloam, no living fountain gladdened the city," three thousand were baptized in a small part of one day. Now what do those who make John take Jerusalem and Judea out to Enon to immerse them because there is much water there? All at once, and very conveniently, there are discovered a number of reservoirs and baths.

But it is forgotten that these can only belong to the rich; and not many rich or mighty were in the habit of befriending the followers of Christ; and the great mass of the converts appear to have been strangers at Jerusalem. Not the least intimation is found that such bathing places were resorted to. And a simple mathematical calculation will show that the eleven apostles could hardly have immersed three thousand persons in so short a time. All these circumstances show a high degree of probability that there was no immersion here.

The jailor (Acts xvi. 19-30) was baptized in the night, and it should seem in prison. But it is urged there might be a bath there; and long arguments are held to show that the prison *might* have been furnished with a bath, in which the jailor *might* have been immersed. Surely, surely, that is a happy facility of discovery, which after making it necessary for all Judea to go out to Jordan to find water enough to be baptized, and to go to a particular point on Jordan,—to Enon, because there is much water there,—can presently find water enough anywhere and everywhere. If a bath should perchance be wanted, there is no difficulty: a stroke of the pen places it there; and a certain immersion is performed without a scrap of evidence in the history to show that an immersion was possible!

But this ground is now very generally given up, and a way for immersion is found out even without a bath in the prison. It is now maintained that they *went forth;* because he was brought out of prison, and then brought into the house; and it is demanded, as an unanswerable argument, why he was taken abroad in the night, except for immersion; or why taken abroad at all, if he might be baptized by sprinkling within.

Now this is to give up the baptism in a bath within the prison; for I take it as a point not to be debated, that he was not baptized both in the prison and out of it, in one and the same baptism. But in letting this stronghold go, as they in justice should, have they found another, where they may rest secure? I think not. The jailor thrust them into the *inner* prison: then he brought them out of that into the more common part of the prison; not out of doors abroad; for we see that he was ready to kill himself when he supposed the prisoners had escaped, even by means of an earthquake. In this prison proper the baptism was performed: then the jailor brought them into his *house; i. e.*, into his dwelling apartments, doubtless attached to the prison. There was no going abroad at all. Paul would not go out upon leave, till the magistrates came and fetched him out. So, the bath is given up, and the substitute fails: and according to the proper rules of argument we should be entitled to have it granted, on their own ground, that here was no immersion. Every expedient has failed, and we have, in all reason, a simple common baptism by sprinkling or pouring.

Paul's baptism is recorded in Acts ix. 17, 18. He

was in his chamber, blind, and weak with fasting three days. "He arose (or stood up) and was baptized; and when he had received meat he was strengthened." What pretence for a bath in this inner chamber? What is there to show that he went abroad in his weak state, before he had received meat and was strengthened? I am unable even to conjecture what. It was, I think, beyond proper question, a baptism by sprinkling or pouring.

The baptism of Cornelius is recorded, Acts x. 44. Those who heard Peter were first baptized with the Holy Ghost. "And as I began to speak, the Holy Ghost *fell* on them, as on us at the beginning. Then remembered I the word of the Lord, how that he said, John indeed baptized with water, but ye shall be baptized with the Holy Ghost," Acts xi. 15. He reasoned at the time thus: These have received the Holy Ghost; can any man forbid water? They have received the greater baptism, can any man forbid the less: they have the reality, can any man forbid the sign? His idea seems to be, not that they might be carried and *applied to the water;* but that *water might be brought* and applied to *them.* The Spirit's mode of baptizing was a falling upon, and such, it seems clearly, was the probable application of the water here.

Here I rest under the second inquiry. Not only is there no evidence that the apostles always baptized by immersion, but clear evidence to the contrary: and I add, no certain evidence that they immersed at all. The probability, even so far as concerns this, is on the other side. I do profess myself unable, and my belief that all other men are unable, to make out a clear case of baptism by immersion in the New Testament. And yet if twenty might be made out, it would not invalidate the argument, as I shall show under the third inquiry.

Previously to entering upon this, however, it seems desirable to say a word, in passing, on the argument FROM HISTORY. This is not indeed essential. I care not who gets the argument from history, provided I get the argument clear and decisive from the word of God.

That immersion was early and extensively practiced is certain. That it was not considered essential is also certain.* The practice was never invariable. The sick and feeble were baptized by affu-

---

* JUSTIN is relied on to prove that immersion only was practiced in his day. But he uses such language as renders it certain that he by no means considered immersion essential; and such as renders it doubtful whether he meant immersion at all. Thus, when he is writing to the Emperor, he invariably describes the baptism, and does not use the word baptize at all. He describes the baptism by the words λουω (louo) "to wash," and λουτρον, "washing." But these words referred to no particular mode of applying water, least of all to an indispensable immersion; and if he thought immersion essential, he wilfully misled the Emperor, who would of necessity understand that they were washed in any mode, and not necessarily immersed; but if in any specific mode—by an application of water to the subject, not of the subject to the water.—*Chapin*, p. 65.

sion or sprinkling; and baptism in such modes was distinctly recognized as valid as in other cases. Novatian was baptized by affusion as he lay upon his bed in sickness. The Emperor Constantine was baptized by Eusebius, of Nicomedia, lying on his bed, clothed in white. Sixty or seventy years after the Apostles, a Jew, while travelling with Christians, fell sick, and desired baptism. Not having water, they sprinkled him thrice with sand. "He recovered. His case was reported to the bishop, who decided that the man was baptized, if only he had water poured on him again."* LAURENTIUS is mentioned as baptizing two persons, Romanus and Lucilius, by affusion. "A little while before he suffered, he baptized one of his executioners with a *pitcher of water.*"† Many such cases are all along incidentally recorded. Upon the best search that I can make, I am compelled to abide by the conclusion of Dr. Pond, who says (p. 43), "I propose it as an indubitable fact that immersion was never considered essential to baptism, till the rise of the Anabaptists in Germany, in the sixteenth century."

History shows that Christians early laid an improper stress upon baptism, attributing to it an efficacy which by no means belongs to it. To the simple rite of baptism by sprinkling or affusion practiced by the Apostles, they soon added a more tho-

---

* Pond, p. 45. † Ibid. p. 48.

rough washing with a greater quantity of water.* And this is scarce to be wondered at when we remember how Peter said, "Lord, not my feet only, but my hands and my head." And yet our Saviour did seem to caution his disciples against this tendency to overdo and overburden religious rites, when he replied, "He that is washed, needeth not, save to wash his feet, but is clean every whit." The tendency was never to throw off any part of the ceremony, but to add more. To immersion they soon added a trine, or threefold immersion; exorcisms (or expelling the devil from the candidate); putting salt on the tongue; anointing the eyes, ears and mouth with spittle; marking with the sign of the cross; clothing in a white robe, and anointing with oil. They went further. Not content with being literally buried in the waters, they imbibed another notion from "putting off the old man," and also from the nakedness of Christ on the cross (for the same passage which speaks of being buried with Christ speaks of the old man being crucified with Christ): and they baptized all naked: men, women, youths, children, all alike, actually naked, divested of all clothing! Truly, "Baptisteries" were necessary at that period: and he would not be wide from the

---

* Jerome speaks of a mode of baptism as common in the ancient church, which was not to dip the whole body, but a "*thrice dipping of the head.*" Augustine mentions the same. (Pond. p. 46.)

mark who should see here a reason for their invention, to remedy the indecencies of the scene; but from the beginning it was not so. For authority as to this fact I refer to Dr. Wall's History of Infant Baptism, and to Dr. Miller on Baptism, p. 105. Wall says, "The ancient Christians, when they were baptized by immersion, were all baptized naked, whether they were men, women or children." Dr. Miller adds, "We have the same evidence (to wit, from history) in favor of immersing divested of all clothing, that we have for immersion at all," and that "so far as the history of the Church subsequent to the Apostolic age informs us, these must stand or fall together."

The argument from history, therefore, proves nothing pertinent to the determining of the question, or it proves altogether too much. It cannot weigh against the word of God, and the suitable exposition of the law of baptism as instituted by Christ.

But here justice requires that I go a little further. A tract entitled "*A Familiar Dialogue between Peter and Benjamin on the subject of Communion,*" is in common and extensive circulation, on the first page of which is the following statement: "As late as 1643, in the Assembly of Divines at Westminster, sprinkling was substituted for immersion by a majority of ONE—25 voted for sprinkling, 24 for immersion. This small majority was obtained by the earnest request of Dr. Lightfoot, who had acquired great influence in that Assembly."

Now all this is told for truth. It is told most circumstantially: "in 1643"—"the Assembly of Divines"—"majority of *one*"—"24 for immersion"—"25 for sprinkling"—"by the earnest request of Dr. Lightfoot."

Like other fictions, this fiction is founded on fact, but it is not the truth.

From the journal of Lightfoot it appears,

1. That the matter in dispute was "*sprinkling being granted, whether dipping* SHOULD BE TOLERATED WITH IT." The proposition, "It is lawful and sufficient to besprinkle the child," had been canvassed and was ready to vote. But Dr. Lightfoot "spoke against it as being very unfit to vote that it is *lawful* to sprinkle when every one grants it." Whereupon it was fallen upon, sprinkling being granted, whether dipping should be tolerated with it. And here, says Lightfoot, "we fell upon a large and long discourse whether dipping was essential, or used in the first institution, or in the Jews' custom."

2. It was not true that 24 voted for immersion, as opposed to sprinkling; but, as Dr. Lightfoot says, "so many were unwilling to have dipping excluded, that the votes came to an equality within one." It was not that they wished immersion to be adopted, or even recommended in the Directory; but simply that the Directory might not prohibit immersion to those who should prefer it. When the proposition was put in such a shape as not to make dipping unlawful, the Assembly, with great unanimity, declared

in their Directory that for the mode of baptizing, it is "*not only lawful, but* ALSO SUFFICIENT, and MOST EXPEDIENT, to be by pouring or sprinkling water on the face of the child, without adding any other ceremony."

3. Nothing at all was finally determined on that vote of 24 to 25. "After that vote," Lightfoot says, "when we had done all, we concluded nothing about it, but the business was recommitted."

On the following points, then, the statement of the tract in question is not true:

1. It is not true, that sprinkling was substituted for immersion by the Assembly of Divines.

2. It is not true, that 24 voted for immersion and 25 for sprinkling, as opposing or preferring sprinkling to immersion. All they wanted was, not to *exclude* dipping as unlawful; and as soon as this point was yielded them, they "with great unanimity" concurred in the vote declaring sprinkling to be "lawful," "sufficient and most expedient."

3. It is not true, that the Assembly finally determined anything as touching this matter by a majority of one.

From this is vamped up the statement in the tract; and the statement is made in such a connection as to lead people to understand, that "immersion" had been the common mode, and the Assembly substituted sprinkling for it. There was no such substitution, either in fact, or even so much as a substitution of the word sprinkling for the word immersion in the Directory. That the statements of the tract are grossly untrue, may be seen by a bare reference to dates, which every schoolboy ought to know.

The *time* when the sprinkling was said to be substituted for immersion was the year 1643. Twenty-three years before this, the Pilgrim Fathers landed at Plymouth; and if immersion had been the common practice in England, they would have brought it with them. But the fact was so far from this, that sixteen years after, Roger Williams removed from Massachusetts to Providence, and continued a Pedobaptist for three years longer. When at length he turned Baptist, as Mr. Hague, the present minister of the original Roger Williams Church in Providence, says, in his "Historical Discourse"—(and as is narrated in the "Life of Roger Williams")—"The difficulty that arose was the want of a proper administrator: for at that time, *no ordained minister could be found in America who had been immersed on a profession of faith*. And yet there were many aged ministers in America, who had long been ministers in Old England before they came across the waters! A Mr. Ezekiel Hariman, a layman, first immersed Mr. Williams, and then Mr. Williams immersed the rest. This was the beginning of the Baptists in America.

From these facts alone any one may see that it cannot possibly be true, that immersion had been the common mode of baptism in England up to 1643, and that sprinkling was then substituted for it, on the authority of the Assembly of Divines.

I need not pursue this matter further: nor indeed was it essential to advert to it at all. If we should grant everything from ecclesiastical history which any desire to assume, it would bear nothing on the question. Christianity in the hands of men may become corrupt; it did early become corrupt. The word of God is the pure fountain. What instructions may be gathered there? To the law, to the testimony. History shows that immersion was not at any time considered by the ancient church as essential to baptism; and if the ancient church had thought it essential, still we have no authority for making that essential which was not deemed so by the apostles and the word of God. I return to the argument.

III. ON THE SUPPOSITION THAT THE EARLY "DISCIPLES ALWAYS BAPTIZED BY IMMERSION, IS THERE EVIDENCE THAT THEY CONSIDERED THAT MODE ESSENTIAL?"

Suppose the command had been, "Let every believer go down from Jerusalem to Jericho." Suppose that the Saviour and his early disciples all went by one particular way, and always rode on ass colts. Must we always go in that road? Must we always ride on ass colts? or is it essential whether we ride at all? Certainly not. We are commanded to go down from Jersusalem to Jericho, and this we must do. But to go in any particular road; or to ride;

or to walk; is no part of the command. The thing is required, the mode is not a matter of command.* He usurps the prerogative of Christ, who makes any particular road, or any particular mode of going, essential.

So here; we are to be baptized, and simply baptized. But I have shown that the words "baptize" and "baptism" were in common use among the Jews at that time to denote a ritual purification by sprinkling or pouring; possibly also they were in use to denote a ritual purification by immersion, though this lacks proof; and were it indubitably proved, still the only effect would be to show that there are three authorized modes of baptizing instead of two; and the argument would be the stronger that the mode is not essential. In this state of the case, suppose Christ and his disciples had all been baptized by sprinkling. This does not bind us to be baptized in that mode. Had they all been baptized by immersion, it would not bind us to an immersion. Here are several modes of applying water, all called equally baptism. Our Lord commands us to be

---

* Thus, we celebrate the Lord's Supper with bread and wine. But Christ and the apostles first celebrated it under the following circumstances, in which nobody deems it essential to follow them. 1. It was at night. 2. In an upper room. 3. They used unleavened bread. 4. They partook in a reclining posture. 5. After eating a meal. 6. With no female disciples present. To my mind there appears just as much reason for insisting on the mode of baptism, as for insisting on the observance of these six particulars in the celebration of the Lord's Supper, and no more.

baptized: the particular mode he does not designate. How can we tell that he did not, for the most consequential reasons, leave it indeterminate? If we add the mode to the command, we add to the law of Christ.

But here it may be replied, "Is there not ONE faith, ONE Lord, ONE BAPTISM?" Indeed, it is much insisted by our Baptist brethren that the *unity* of baptism consists in *unity of mode;* and that three modes, sprinkling, pouring, immersing, make three baptisms.

I might here be entitled to insist, that if the unity of baptism consists in unity of mode, then the mode of immersion is most certainly excluded; for *sprinkling* has been proved a lawful mode; and *pouring*, by its superior proof, comes in with a better title than immersion, even if sprinkling were given up.

But the unity of baptism does not consist in the unity of mode, but *in the unity of design*, the unity of *signification*, unity with regard to the great truths to which it refers; unity into the "one body into which we are all baptized by the same Spirit."

The Bible unequivocally teaches us that the one baptism does not consist in the *one mode*. Turn to Acts xix. Certain disciples had been ignorantly baptized with John's baptism, instead of the baptism which Christ enjoined, and were baptized over again. I am aware that many of our Baptist brethren think it necessary to insist that there was no re-baptism: and it is scarce a wonder; because if there was here a re-baptism it effectually shows that John's baptism and Christian baptism are entirely distinct; and spoils many arguments founded on the notion that the baptisms are the same. Thus, in the tract that has already been quoted,—the "Familiar Dialogue between Peter and Benjamin," published by the "Baptist General Tract Society" (p. 5), Peter is made to say in the dialogue,—"I have been a little puzzled with the account given in Acts xix. 1-6, respecting the disciples whom Paul found at Ephesus. Do you think they were re-baptized?" Benjamin is made to answer,—"By no means, and I think I can relieve your mind in a few words;" and then goes on to argue that there was no re-baptism. I only wonder that a cause, which requires so plain a statement of Scripture to be denied, should be thought worth defending. The words of the Scripture are these: "And he said unto them, *unto what were ye then baptized? And they said, unto John's baptism.* Then said Paul, John verily baptized with the baptism of repentance, saying unto the people that they should believe on him which should come after him; that is, on Christ Jesus. *When they heard this, they were baptized in the name of the Lord Jesus.* And when Paul had laid his hands upon them, the Holy Ghost came on them."*

---

* Mr. Carson admits, p. 372, that in Acts xix. 1-6, some who had been baptized with John's baptism were baptized

Hard lot, indeed, to be driven to deny that here was a re-baptism, and yet to hold on to the scheme that requires such a denial!

But mark: here were two baptisms, while there need not have been more than one mode. *Unity of mode, therefore, does not make unity of baptism;* AND UNITY OF BAPTISM DOES NOT CONSIST IN THE MODE; it lies in something else. Here the mode was good enough; but the design, the intent, the truths on the faith of which the baptism was based, were different. These made the two transactions in one mode, two baptisms. The "one baptism," therefore, consists in the one design, the one signification, the unity of faith in the same truths which are represented by baptism; and ONENESS *in these things* would make ONE BAPTISM, though the mere outward modes should vary ever so much; and the mode is not essential. To make the unity of baptism consist in the mode is, as if we were to make a man's identify consist in his dress; he is one man in a coat with broad skirts; he is quite another man, and has lost all his legal and social and personal identity, in a coat with narrow skirts.

And mark still further here: in the main particulars, the essentials, of the baptism with which Christ was baptized, we are *not to follow him;* and so

---

over again. "I know this is disputed," he says, "but for my part I never doubted it. I cannot see how this can be denied, without torturing the word of God."

another set of arguments and of strong appeals falls to the ground.

He was not baptized *till thirty years old*, and that for a special reason. We are not to follow him here.

He was not baptized "*unto repentance.*" John's disciples could not follow him here.

He was not baptized to "*wash away sins.*" No man can follow him here.

He was not baptized in the "*name of the Son and of the Holy Ghost.*" No man is to follow him here.

In fine: according to the word of God, if we had been baptized with John's baptism ever so ceremoniously, in order to Christian baptism we must needs be baptized over again.

I go on with the argument. Now our Lord commanded us simply to be baptized: and there being in common use *two* (or if we grant our Baptist brethren, what we do not desire to deny, but what they cannot prove,—*three*) modes of ritual purifying called baptism; our Lord left the mode indeterminate. How can we tell that he did not with deliberation and for the most consequential reasons, leave it indeterminate?

Suppose you make the mode essential, and insist that all shall be immersed, or barred out of the Church. How can you tell that you are not presuming to require what the Lord purposely left optional for the most cogent and essential reasons? And if so, how will you answer it to God for attempting thus to judge "another man's servant," and to "lord it over God's heritage?" Suppose that Christ forbore to enjoin the particular mode of immersion for this reason: to wit—that his Gospel is designed to fill the whole earth, and to be applicable with all its ordinances to all men everywhere in all conditions. But there are deserts, where men may travel for days and not find water enough for immersion. There are frozen regions, where immersion is a large part of the year nearly or quite impracticable. Many are sick; many are in such a state of health that they cannot go abroad, much less be immersed, especially in winter, without endangering their lives. Must all these be kept from Christ's ordinances, because some think that what Christ saw fit (perhaps for these very reasons among others) not to prescribe, should be made essential? Because these cannot be immersed, are they therefore to linger and die without ever partaking of the Lord's Supper, whatever their desire for that and for baptism, too?

It has been well said that "baptism was made for man, not man for baptism;" and may not Christ have designedly left the mode undetermined for such reasons as these? Is there no presumption in adding the mode to his command? Or, waiving these considerations, and supposing that, in Judea, immersion might always have been readily practiced on account of the comparative mildness of the climate; and granting, moreover, that nobody was ever sick there; can we be sure that it is entirely in keeping with the simplicity of Christ, and with the lightness and simplicity of his ordinances, to— cut a hole in the ice, and immerse sixty men and women, while the weather is so cold as to keep a number of men employed in stirring the water with poles to keep it from freezing over while the immersion is going on?—as the papers have informed us was done in the Delaware river the last winter. Since Christ has not commanded this, nor required baptism to be done in the mode of immersion at all, how can we dare to add such doings as these to his gentle and easy commands?

We cannot. We dare not. And yet for this we must be cut off from communion with those whom we love as brethren. We see no scriptural evidence for the peculiar mode of immersion: but we leave our brethren to decide for themselves according to their conscience. We have conscientiously intended to obey the command to be baptized. We think we have obeyed it. But our brethren judge over our consciences, and would thrust us from the church, unless we will submit our judgment and our conscience to theirs. They often say to us, "Since you regard immersion as valid baptism, you ought to come to us, since we cannot in conscience come to you." We reply, Brethren, can you not allow us liberty of conscience, too? Can you not receive us without stripping us of our dearest rights? We are ready to allow and give immersion to them; but we demand liberty of conscience, too. We are required to come under a yoke which we are confident Christ never imposed. We are required to do that which we consider is adding to Christ's commands; thrusting out many from his ordinances; and compelling many more to enjoy them at the risk of their lives. Nay, if we would yield our own consciences and surrender our own liberty, they would then compel us, in the same manner, to lord it over the consciences of others; or, in default, cast us out of the church: and so, if the Baptist were the only church, all those whose earnest research and whose honest conscience should not lead them to see immersion, and only immersion, in all the baptisms of the New Testament, must be debarred from Christ's house on earth, and excommunicated from his table! And every one who will consent to join them, is, perforce, compelled to join in this unhallowed proscription of the children of God and heirs of salvation; and that under penalty of discipline and censure, even to excommunication! A man may not commune at Christ's table, even with his own father, or with the wife of his bosom, be they ever so faithful to Christ, if they are so unfortunate as not to see immersion in baptism, and have been baptized in any other mode! No—everything must be squared to *their* understanding, and cut according to *their* opinion. The wife shall be debarred from partaking of the emblems of the body and the blood of the Saviour in connection with her dying husband, who desires once more, before he departs, to commemorate a Saviour's love!

We feel not at liberty to countenance such a ruthless despotism as this. Could we surrender our own liberty, we have yet some conscience left which forbids us to lend our aid in tyrannizing over the consciences of others. Had we personally no objection to immersion, we should feel bound, for freedom's sake, for the truth's sake, and for Christ's sake, to "stand fast in that liberty wherewith Christ hath made us free." We are not willing to be made the instruments of destroying the liberty of others. As we love Christ we dare not be brought under such a "yoke of bondage to any man." As we love God, or regard the rights of men, we dare not join in this unhallowed lording it over the consciences of others. We remember that it is written, "Who art thou, that judgeth another man's servant? To his own master he standeth or falleth." We leave it to every man's conscience to decide whether he has been baptized; and when he is satisfied that according to his own understanding and his own conscience he has obeyed the command to be baptized, we dare not judge him. On the customary tokens of piety, and on the customary profession, as that custom exists in churches of any other evangelical denomination, we receive him, and with open arms, to our communion, and to that table which is not ours, but the Lord's.*

But when we have seen on what ground exclusive immersion is required; when—as we are required to prove all things—we *prove* it by the word of God, and in our sober judgment, its very foundations flit away "like the baseless fabric of a vision;" how can we on such grounds join in unchurching and cut-

---

* "There were at that time (1689), several churches of Calvinistic Baptists, who held to open communion, especially in Bedfordshire, where John Bunyan preached." (Murdock's Mosheim, Vol. iii., p. 540.)

"Before the erection of regular Baptist congregations, and indeed for some time after, it was very common for Baptists and others to belong to the same church, and to worship and commune together." (Ibid., p. 541.)

The celebrated Robert Hall was most strenuously opposed to close communion.

Our Baptist brethren are fond of saying that they hold to no more close communion than we do. Will they put it to the test? Will they receive to their communion every person who has, on a credible profession of piety, been received to some evangelical church of another denomination, and who, "according to his own understanding, and his own conscience, has obeyed the command to be baptized?"

We give the following invitation before the communion: "Members of other churches present, of all evangelical denominations, in regular standing in their own churches, are invited to partake with us." If our Baptist brethren hold to no more close communion than we, will they adopt this form? If not, will they give up their assertion as fallacious and untrue?

ting off from the communion of the saints so many others, who, we cannot doubt, are received of God? No, we have not so learned Christ. We have gone to His word for our views of truth and order. On that we rest. Leaving it to others to answer their own conscience, and to enjoy their belief without let or molestation from us, on the ground which we have examined and proved we stand fast. If our views of faith and order should be assailed, we shall nevertheless remember, that we have examined and proved them; and, with much prayer, and with solemn and full conviction, have found that they rest broadly and solidly upon the eternal word of God.

III.

ADDITIONAL DISSERTATIONS UPON PARTICULAR POINTS TOUCHING THE INTERPRETATION OF THE WORD BAPTIZE.

I. THE CLASSIC GREEK AND THE GREEK OF THE NEW TESTAMENT.

Says Professor Robinson, in his preface to his Lexicon of the New Testament:

"A Lexicon of the New Testament, at the present day, presupposes the fact, that the language of the New Testament exhibits in many points a departure from the idiom of the Attic Greek. This great question, which so long agitated the learned philologists of Europe, would seem at present to be put entirely at rest." The plan of his lexicon, he says, is, "In defining words, those significations are placed first which accord with Greek usage;" "Then follow those significations which depart from Greek usage, and which are to be either illustrated from the Greek or the Septuagint, as compared with the Hebrew, *or depend solely on the usus loquendi*"

PRINCIPLES OF INTERPRETATION.   101

(customary use of words), "*of the New Testament writers.*"

Dr. George Campbell, whom our Baptist brethren are fond of complimenting as one of the most finished Greek scholars of modern times, maintains that many of the idioms of the New Testament Greek would not have been more intelligible to a classic Greek author than Arabic or Persian. "Take," says he, "the following for examples. Ουκ αδυνατησει παρα τῳ Θεῳ παν ρημα, Luke i. 37; and ουκ αν εσωθη πασα σαρξ, Matt. xxiv. 22." (In English, "With God nothing shall be impossible," and "There should no flesh be saved.") "These passages in the New Testament Greek are," says Campbell, "phrases which, in my apprehension, would not have been more intelligible to a Greek author than Arabic or Persian would have been. Pημα for *thing*, and πασα ουκ for *no one*, or *none*, σαρξ for *person*, etc., would to him, I suspect, have proved insurmountable obstacles." ... "This," says he, "is but a small specimen—not the hundredth part of what might be produced on this subject." (Prelim. Dis. I., vol. i., p. 30.)

"It is true," says Campbell (Prelim. Dis. I. part 2), "that as the New Testament is written in Greek, it must be of consequence that we be able to enter critically into the ordinary import of the words of that tongue." "But from what has been observed, it is evident, that though in several cases this knowledge may be eminently useful, *it will not suffice;* nay, in many cases, it will be of little or no signifi-

9*

cancy." "Classical use, both in Greek and in Latin, is not only, in this study, sometimes unavailable, but *may even mislead. The sacred use and the classical are often very different.*"

The Biblical Repository, for April, 1841, has an article on "*The Bible and its Literature,*" by Professor Edward Robinson. In this article Professor Robinson says, "The language of the New Testament is the latter Greek, as spoken by foreigners of the Hebrew stock, and applied by them to subjects on which it had never been employed by native Greeks. After the disuse of the ancient Hebrew in Palestine, and the irruption of Western conquerors, the Jews adopted the Greek language from necessity;—partly as a conquered people, and partly from intercourse of life and commerce, in colonies, in cities, founded like Alexandria, and others, which were peopled with throngs of Jews. It was, therefore, the spoken language of ordinary life which they learned, not the classic style of books which have elsewhere come down to us. But they spoke it as foreigners, whose native tongue was the latter Aramean; and it therefore could not fail to acquire from their lips a strong Semitic character and coloring. When to this we add, that they spoke in Greek *on the things of the true God, and the relations of mankind to Jehovah and to a Saviour—subjects to which no native Greek had ever applied his beautiful language*—it will be obvious that an APPEAL MERELY TO CLASSIC GREEK AND ITS PHILOLOGY WILL NOT SUF-

FICE FOR THE INTERPRETER OF THE NEW TESTAMENT. *The Jewish-Greek must be studied almost as an independent dialect, etc.*"

The change of meaning in many words of the Greek language, upon adapting it to the ideas and observances of a revealed religion, was a matter of necessity: and that aside from the natural influence of the Hebraic idiom. Carry the Gospel to China, or Hindostan, or among the tribes of our American Indians; it brings them a multitude of ideas which are peculiar to revealed religion. To express these ideas, the old words of their language must receive a new meaning, or they must coin new words; or they must adopt words from the language of those who brought them the new religion, or from some other quarter.*

If, instead of a new *religion*, a new *language* is carried among a people professing the true religion, the words of that new language receive a new meaning the moment they are applied to the religious ideas and observances to which the language was before a stranger. Carry any heathen language into a Gospel land, or into a land of Hebrew rites, and of Hebrew ideas concerning the true God and revealed religion, and it is impossible that the mean-

---

* Said David Brainerd, "There are no words in the Indian language to answer to our English words, Lord, Saviour, salvation, sinner, justice, condemnation, faith, adoption, glory, with scores of like importance."

ing of such words as are applied to these new ideas should not be even more changed than is the idiom of the language in the construction of phrases. Such is the fact with regard to the New Testament Greek as compared with the classic, or even with the common dialect which prevailed after the conquests of Alexander.

A Baptist writer has attempted to explain this matter by referring to the "Irish-English" of an "Irishman, after having become acquainted with our language, and able to speak it with fluency; yet you can detect them using phrases and words peculiar to their own vernacular tongue, and dissimilar to ours." This by no means meets the case, but is calculated entirely to mislead. The Irishman has religious ideas, to a great extent common with us. An African or an Indian might learn our language, and yet speak it in a manner peculiar to himself. But what would be the effect upon their *own* language, when the Christian religion was once completely established among them? New ideas fill the mind of the benighted pagan, and lift up his thoughts to angels—to Heaven—to God. He thinks of redemption, of faith, of holiness. His thoughts, his hopes, his intellect, his heart,—all are wonderfully transformed. "Old things pass away: all things become new." Are his lips sealed? Is he dumb? Are African converts never to speak to each other of the kingdom of God? The words of their language remaining the same, and applied to these new and wonderful

PRINCIPLES OF INTERPRETATION. 105

ideas, is their meaning the same? Is the whole change expressed by referring to the brogue of an Irishman whose mother tongue was Irish-English, and whose ideas have never changed from pagan to Christian?

That such was the effect of adapting the pagan Greek language to the Christian religion, any one may see, who will sit down patiently and turn over the leaves of a Lexicon of the New Testament, which adequately discriminates and marks the transition.

The sole intent of all this discussion about the classic use and the New Testament use, is to show that the word baptize in the New Testament *may have left its primary classic signification*, and have received a GENERIC, SACRED use, *equivalent to* WASHING *or* PURIFYING, *without the least reference to the mode in which that "washing of water" is performed*. Whether this be the fact or not, is to be learned not from the Greek classics, but from the New Testament itself. As to this matter of fact, Mark and Luke and Paul are better witnesses concerning what they themselves understood by the word baptize, than Xenophon, Aristotle, or than even that Hebrew of Hebrews, the Jewish Josephus, when he is using the word in the sense of the Greek classics, with no reference to its use as applied to a religious ordinance.

Will any Baptist make an issue on this poir t, and maintain that Apostles and Evangelists are not to be heard in evidence? Will any Baptist maintain that Evangelists and Apostles may not explain their own meaning in just the same way that heathen Greeks may explain theirs? Will any Baptist maintain, that where the testimony of the New Testament writers differs from that of the heathen Greeks, the New Testament witness is not to be heard before any heathen, and before all the heathen classics together? In fine, the question here is, *Is the Holy Ghost a competent and credible witness as to the sense in which the Holy Ghost uses the word baptize?*

JUDD ON MARK VII. 4.

Mr. Judd, in his reply to Stuart, p. 25, translates the passage, "And when they come from the market, except they βαπτισωνται, baptize themselves." In the same manner he makes the Pharisee, in Luke xi. 38, wonder that Jesus had not baptized before dinner. As Mr. Judd maintains that baptize must and shall mean immerse, he maintains that baptize not only may have its usual meaning here, but that "that meaning is absolutely required by the scope and harmony of the passage:" *i. e.*, he will make the Scripture here testify that the Pharisees and all the Jews immersed their whole bodies before eating, as often as they came from the market. "Surely," says he, p. 37, "the Jews could have immersed themselves after coming from the market." Surely they *could*, if they never went from the market, and took their meals where they *could not*. But Mr. Judd mistakes the question. The inquiry should be, not whether they surely could immerse themselves, but whether they surely did. It is not necessary to show that the act of immersion was physically impossible: the proper inquiry is, not whether it was impossible to be done, but whether it can possibly be true that it *was actually done*. Surely the Jews could have eaten Stephen like cannibals after they had stoned him; for the thing was not impossible to be done: but it was impossible that it should be true that it was done. Of such a custom of immersing the whole body as often as they came from the market, there is not a scrap of evidence in the wide world, except in the assumed meaning of the word baptize. The manners and customs of the Jews have been well known; and no such custom was ever known or heard of, till invented as a historical fact necessary to help the Baptists out of this difficulty.

DR. GEORGE CAMPBELL ON MARK VII. 4, AND LUKE XI. 38.

The learned George Campbell, whom our Baptist brethren are so fond of quoting on these passages, in Mark vii. 4, and Luke xi. 38, finds it impossible to carry out his theory. He is about the work of translating the New Testament: and he is determined beforehand that baptize must mean exclusively immerse.

Mark says, that the "Pharisees and all the Jews, when they come from the market, except they baptize themselves, eat not." Mr. Campbell does not believe that they *immersed themselves* as often as they came from the market. What does he do? Does he give a grammatical and faithful translation of the word baptize? He dares not. He gives no translation: he makes a gloss: he gives a commentary, and corrects and alters the diction of the Scriptures by substituting his comment in the place of the words which the Holy Ghost teacheth. And this is his comment—for no scholar, I trust, will ever venture to call it a translation. "For the Pharisees, and indeed all the Jews, who observe the tradition of the elders, eat not except they have washed their hands by POURING A LITTLE WATER UPON THEM!" The words, "by pouring a little water upon them," are not in the original; they are inserted by Mr. Campbell. And, in the name of wonder, I would demand, does the word Νιπτω (*Nipto*) necessarily limit the mode of washing to "pouring a little water on the hands?" Does it not mean to *wash;* and *simply* "wash;" without referring in the least to the mode; whether by pouring the water on the hands, or by dipping them? But let us go on with Mr. Campbell's translation: "For the Pharisees, and indeed all the Jews who observe the traditions of the elders, eat not except they have washed their hands by *pouring a little water upon them:* and when they come from the market, by DIPPING THEM." Does he call this a *translation* of the words μη βαπτισωνται? Does the verb *baptizo* then mean, TO DIP THE HANDS? I repeat it: a comment this may be; but it is no simple nor faithful translation of the word of God. Nor can a faithful translation of the passage be made, giving to "baptize" the meaning of "immerse," without making the passage speak that which Mr. Campbell held as not true. Carson is right, and must have the judgment of every unbiased scholar in his favor, that Campbell's notion of making this baptism refer to the hands by dipping them, is "an ingenious device, without any authority from the genius and practice of the language."

Campbell's translation of Luke xi. 38 is still more remarkable. Luke, inspired by the Holy Ghost, says, "The Pharisee marvelled that Jesus had not first *been baptized* before dinner" (εβαπτισθη). Which Campbell thus translates: "But the Pharisee was surprised to observe that he USED NO WASHING before dinner." Here the distinction between washing and dipping cannot be pretended: and what becomes of Campbell's argument about "immerse" as being the only proper meaning of the word "baptize?" Here the Scripture says, "The Pharisee marvelled that Jesus had not been *baptized* before dinner." Campbell dares not translate the word "baptize" here by the word "immerse:" nor does he find it possible to introduce the word "hands!" The first would make the Bible speak falsehood, and the latter would be too gross "an alteration of the diction of the Holy Ghost." He therefore gives up all talk about immersing or dipping—and says, "He used NO WASHING before dinner," and so is, after all, driven on to the very ground adopted in our common English translation.

PROFESSOR RIPLEY ON MARK VII. 4, AND LUKE XI. 38.

The remarks of Professor Ripley on these two passages, in his examination of Professor Stuart, are, it seems to me, as curious a piece of non-committal, and of tripping lightly over ground on which one dares not tread firmly, as can be found in the whole compass of Biblical criticism.

He thinks the passage in Mark may be rendered, "without the least violence to its language," so as to make it read that the Pharisees and all the Jews immerse their whole bodies as often as they come from the market.

"May be rendered!" "without violence to the language!" Is that proper reading? Is that the truth, concerning what was customarily done by the Jews upon coming from the market? Does Professor Ripley believe that such a custom was so universal and so invariable among the Jews, as to make it a wonder, that Jesus should sit down to dinner without having first immersed his whole body? Hear him. "That some of the stricter sort, that many, enough to justify the Evangelist's general expression, did practice total ablution on the occasion mentioned, is altogether credible." *Some— of the stricter sort!—many!* enough to *justify* the Evangelist!—is altogether *credible!* Then Professor Ripley dares not join, without misgiving, in affirming that "*all* the Jews" had the custom of immersing themselves when they came from the market? No. He says, "In the absence of clear satisfying proof, it is not becoming to make positive assertions." How is this? The word "baptize" mean exclusively "immerse;"—the Holy Ghost affirm that they baptize themselves;—and yet no "clear satisfying proof" that they immerse themselves! Is the witness not a credible one, or is there some doubt whether the word means "immerse?"

But Professor Ripley says he is by no means satisfied that this is a "necessary view of the passage," viz., that they immerse themselves. "*Necessary!*" Will he hold to it at all? We shall see.

But says he again, "However striking the language of Mark may, by some, be considered, as recognizing such a practice (and the language is certainly coincident with such a practice, especially when we look at it by the investigations respecting "baptize" on the preceding pages), yet I am not disposed to urge it." Not diposed to urge it? Does he believe it? Will he venture to stand upon that ground? Will he venture either to affirm it or deny it? No—he dares not rest upon either ground, and make the Bible read either "except they immerse themselves," or "except they immerse their hands." He gently feels the ground of the first with his foot, but dares not venture upon it. He then poises himself, and presses with the other foot upon other ground; but he dares not rest upon this and abandon the first. With regard to the first he says, "In the absence of clear, satisfying proof, it is not becoming to make any positive assertions;" "the language is coincident with such a practice;" "it *may* be so rendered without the least violence;" "yet I am not disposed to urge it." With regard to the second he says, "But assuming the ground, that the evangelist did not intend to distinguish a total bathing from a partial washing, I again inquire did he distinguish one sort of partial washing from another sort of partial washing, one of which sorts was performed by dipping the hands into water?" And yet, assuming this ground, he assumes it only to argue: he reaches back to the other, and reminds us again that he has already said that the word βαπτισωνται in this passage, "MAY WITHOUT ANY VIOLENCE" be considered as distinguishing a total immersion from a washing of the hands. Thus he will venture forward to argue upon one ground, provided he may keep open a safe retreat to the other. How firmly he may feel the ground under him may be inferred by his evident concern to keep open a retreat to the ground on which, alas, he is afraid to stand; and concerning which he admits that there is an "absence of clear, satisfying proof."

Standing thus with light and uncertain tread upon both grounds, he is compelled to make the Bible give an uncertain sound: and while professing to fix the sense with critical accuracy, he actually proposes to make it read, in both passages, with an ALIAS. After the word "baptize" (wash) in Mark vii. 5 (which he would read "immerse, or bathe"), he says, "The word *hands* may be considered as understood, or the word *themselves* may be understood." There is an "absence of clear, satisfying proof" that they immersed themselves; and he is not certain that they simply immersed their hands. So he would split the difference by making the Bible read both ways, putting in an *alias*. In the same manner, in Luke xi. 38, he proposes the introduction of the same double reading for one single word. "And when the Pharisee saw it, he marvelled that he had not first washed before dinner: that he had not first IMMERSED; that is, himself, OR his hands."

I have some fault to find with Professor Ripley's criticism, on the score of grammatical accuracy; for this, too, it appears to me, he has sacrificed on the altar of exclusive immersion.

Says Professor Ripley, "The verb (βαπτισωνται) is in the middle voice; and as there is no object expressed after it, it would be *lawful*, in order to express the Greek, to employ, as Professor Stuart has, the word *themselves*, as being contained in the verb itself." This is correct, save that instead of simply being lawful to do as Professor Stuart has done, it is indispensable to do so, unless you can translate it by an English word, which, like the Greek middle voice of a transitive verb, has a reflexive sense, implying that the agent is himself both the subject and the object of the verb. Thus, if we say, "Except they *wash*"—the meaning is except they wash *themselves:* or if we say, "Except they *bathe*"—the object of the bathing is still *themselves*. But in what follows, it appears to me that Professor Ripley is most palpably and indefensibly in the wrong. He says, "As the verb νιψωνται (wash), in the former part of the passage, has, in the middle voice, an object (χειρας—hands) after it, it is certainly justifiable to maintain, that the verb in the latter part of the passage (βαπτισωνται) has the same word understood after it for its object."

Now the middle voice does indeed admit an object after it, as in the case of νιψωνται. It would therefore have been justifiable for the writer to have placed an object after βαπτισωνται—*had his meaning allowed it*. But when the writer omits the object in such a case, and the meaning of the word is still reflexive, the subject of the verb is its implied object. When the writer in such a case omits to express another object, we pervert his meaning, if we understand or supply an object other than the one implied in the very form of the verb, which makes its object identical with its agent. Thus Professor

Stuart has most grammatically read the word βαπ-τισωνται (Baptisontai) "they wash themselves." And it certainly is *not* "justifiable;" it is a flagrant violation of the rules of grammar, to supply, as Professor Ripley has done, the word *hands*, instead of themselves.

In Luke xi. 38, the word is in the passive voice. It not only has not the word "hands" after it, but does not admit the word to be supplied as its object. The grammatical rendering is, "that he had not *been baptized*." The passage in Mark vii. 4, shows that, under such circumstances, people baptized themselves (they did it for themselves; they were not baptized by others). Hence, it is doing justice to the meaning, to say, without being tied down to grammatical nicety, "that he had not first *washed*," or "that he had not first *washed himself*." This does not change the object concerning which the baptism is affirmed. But to supply the word *hands*, as Professor Ripley proposes, is to take an unwarrantable license. It does violence to the grammatical construction, and changes the object of the affirmation. It is quite as gross a violation of grammatical usage, as though the passage were made to read in English, "That he had not first been baptized his hands."* I will only add, that the word hands

---

* Where the accusative is put, by synecdoche, after the passive voice, it limits the action of the verb to the *part* expressed by that accusative. If the writer means so to limit his meaning, he always supplies the accusative; if he does

is not in this passage, or near it. The word baptize used alone and simply, as it is here used by Luke, has no inherent quality by which it should be thought to be limited in the action which it expresses to the hands alone. The word "hands" is *imported* through the channel of commentary; and commentary elaborated, as I think I have shown, by a process of bad criticism.

BAPTIST MISSIONARY TRANSLATIONS.

Our Baptist brethren claim that " to them is committed the sole guardianship of pure and faithful translations of the oracles of God into the languages of the earth."* I should like to know how their foreign translations of these two passages, Mark vii. 4, and Luke xi. 38, read. Do they make the Pharisees and all the Jews *immerse themselves* as often as they come from the market? or do they make *them simply dip their hands?* Which of these two

---

not, he who adds that accusative alters the meaning of the writer. The license is altogether unwarrantable. In the present case, such an addition is a flagrant alteration of, and addition to, the word of God.

Mr. Carson himself, on grammatical grounds, rejects the gloss of those who would supply the word hands in this passage and in Mark vii. 4. He says, p. 78, " When no part is mentioned or excepted, the whole body is always meant."

* American and Foreign Bible Society Report, 1840, p. 79.

acts do our Baptist brethren—"the sole guardians of pure and faithful translations"—teach the heathen is the baptism which the Holy Ghost speaks of in Mark vii. 4? Do they teach the heathen to believe that the Pharisee marvelled that the Saviour had not immersed himself before dinner; or that he had not dipped his hands before dinner? Methinks the "guardians of pure and faithful translations"* should agree in this matter. Infallibility should not be divided; and where it is so, the division shows that neither party is infallible. The truth may lie on neither side.

With these coadjutors, Campbell and Woolsey on my right hand, and Carson and Judd on my left, I should like to go and knock at the door of the

---

* Says Professor Eaton, in his speech before the Baptist Bible Society, at their anniversary (Report of American and Foreign Bible Society, p. 79), "Never, sir, was there a chord struck that vibrated simultaneously through so many Baptist hearts, from one extremity of the land to the other, as when it was announced that the heathen world must look to them alone for an unveiled view of the glories of the Gospel of Christ." "A deep conviction seized the minds of almost the whole body that they were divinely and peculiarly set for the defence and dissemination of the Gospel, as delivered to men by its Heavenly Author. A new zeal in their Master's cause, and unwonted kindlings of fraternal love glowed in their hearts; and an attracting and concentrating movement, reaching to the utmost extremity of the mass, began, and has been going on, and increasing in power ever since."

Baptist Foreign Missionary establishments, and inquire—Brethren, how do you translate the word of God? If they answer—"We make the Bible say that the Pharisees and all the Jews *immerse themselves* as often as they come from the market," then Campbell and Woolsey shall reply—"Brethren, this is not right; you make the word of God speak falsehood." If the missionaries answer—"We make the Bible say that the Pharisees and all the Jews *dip their hands* simply, when they come from the market," then the brethren on my left shall reply, Carson and Judd shall make answer—"Brethren, the word of God says that the Pharisees and all the Jews *immerse themselves*, before eating, as often as they come from the market, and you have given no faithful translation. You have corrupted the word of God. You have corrected and altered the diction of the Holy Ghost." From the sword of the brethren—either of those on my right hand or of those on my left, the missionary translators cannot escape. And now having proved the missionary translation unfaithful—the brethren on my right and the brethren on my left shall turn their arms against each other.* These shall demonstrate that those have

---

* Professor Eaton, of Hamilton Baptist Institute, in his speech before the Baptist Bible Society, at their anniversary in 1840 [See Report of said Society, p. 74], says, "The translation" of the Baptist Missionaries "is so undeniably correct," that its incorrectness could not be "pretended,"

made the Bible speak falsehood; those shall demonstrate that these have disguised and corrupted the word of God. Neither can resist the assault of the other: each scheme is certainly and totally destroyed. And when the battle is fought, in which I have nothing to do but to stand still and wait the issue—when the battle it fought, till each party is so beaten that he can fight no longer; I would take them by the hand, and say, "Brethren, abandon the ground on which you must mutually destroy each

"without committing the objector's character for scholarship and candor." "Who are they, sir," said he, "who cavil upon the plain meaning of the original word whose translation is so offensive? Are they the Porsons, and the Campbells, and the Greenfields, and such like?" "No, sir," —"But the cavillers, sir, are men who, whatever may be their standing in other respects, have no reputation as linguists and philologists to lose. There really can be no rational doubt in the mind of any sound and candid Greek scholar, about the evident meaning of the words in question. I venture to say, at the risk of the little reputation for Greek scholarship which I possess, that there are no words of plainer import in the Bible. The profane tampering which has been applied to these words," etc., etc.

I shall not dispute here, that all this may be very modest and catholic. It is at least such matter as the American and Foreign Bible Society (Baptist) are willing to append to their report, and publish to the world. But I should like to see which side Professor Eaton would take amid these combatants; and in what plight he would stand when the battle is over, take which side he would.

other, or else fight on for ever. Do you not see that each is defenceless in his own position, and irresistble when he attacks that of the other? Between you both the truth comes out clear; that baptism is not necessarily immersion; and that while you endeavor to make it so, you are on the one hand compelled to make the Bible speak falsehood, and on the other, to alter and corrupt the word of God."

And what shall they do? Shall they make peace on the only rational ground? Or shall one yield his judgment to the other, and *vote* that one opinion to be infallible? Or, for the sake of saving the Baptist cause, shall they strike hands and be made friends: agreeing, on the one party, to allow the Bible to speak falsehood, provided it may only speak immersion; and agreeing, on the other party, provided immersion may be retained, to admit the word of God to be altered, and disguised and corrupted, by "an ingenious conceit, without any authority from the practice of the language" in which the New Testament was written?

I would respectfully ask our Baptist brethren to look into this matter. I would respectfully call their attention to the necessity laid upon them in their present position, of falling upon one of the three points of the alternative, which here presents itself to them. With their present disagreement, in which a part of them side with Carson and Judd, and a part with Campbell and Woolsey, it is impossible for them to give a faithful translation, on the Baptist principle, without entering into a compromise, which shall either make the Bible speak falsehood, or else alter and pervert the sacred diction of the word of God. I would respectfully suggest to the brethren of each of these two parties, the necessity of looking into these foreign translations; and of taking heed, lest in their zeal to maintain immersion, they unconsciously fall into such a compromise as this. It surely becomes them to whom " is committed the sole guardianship of pure and faithful translations of the oracles of God, into the languages of the earth," to be careful and uncompromising here.

SCRIPTURAL IDEA OF BAPTISM.

For giving a definition to "baptize" which shall refer to the intent and the import, and omit all reference to the mode—a definition which shall express the substance of baptism, with no reference to the circumstance—we have the soundest warrant and the most explicit example in the word of God. Thus: Jesus, with his disciples, was baptizing in Judea; John in Enon (John iii. 22-26). A question arose between some of John's disciples and the Jews "about PURIFYING." To settle it, they come and refer it to John under the shape of a question about "BAPTIZING." Their minds fastened on the substance, not on the circumstance. Their idea of baptism was not the modern Baptist idea. Baptism with them was not an immersing, but a purifying.

Their question is about baptizing; but it is not about dipping, or sprinkling, or pouring, or immersing, but about PURIFYING: and they state the question to John as a question about *baptizing.* In their view the words "baptize" and "purify" are so far synonymous, that in a debate about purifying, they may use either the word purify or the word baptize. But with them the word purify could not be synonymous with immerse: for their common purifications of persons were either in the general mode of *washing*, or in the particular mode of *sprinkling*—never necessarily in the mode of immersing.

So again in Mark vii. 4, there is a talk about baptizing; and whatever was done, Mr. Woolsey justly maintains was done by the use of the "water-pots." But John ii. 6, speaks of these water-pots as set "after the manner of the *purifying* of the Jews." Here, too, baptism is not an immersion in fact, much less in the idea. The idea of baptism here is not a mere mode of applying water—certainly not the mode of immersion, but a *purifying.*

So again in Luke xi. 38, 39, upon the Pharisee's wondering that Jesus had not been *baptized* before dinner, our Lord took occasion to say to him, "Ye Pharisees make clean (in the original, PURIFY) the outside." Here neither the Saviour nor the Pharisee considered the essence of the baptism as lying in the mode, but in the intent and in the import. Baptism, in their view, was a washing or purifying.

So again in the Apocrypha, Judith xii. 7, it is said

that Judith went out into the valley of Bethulia and *washed* (Sept. *baptized herself*) in the camp (επι της πηγης) AT (not in) a fountain of water in the camp. The context shows that the object of this baptizing was to remove a ceremonial uncleanness. "She without doubt strictly obeyed the law, and did what the law intended that she should do. But the law in such cases simply commanded washing" (Lev. xv.). The narrator does not intend to signify that she went beyond the law, but that she observed it: and in his view *wash* is synonymous with *baptize* in denoting a religious ordinance—a ceremonial purification.

So in Ecclesiasticus xxiv. 25, the words *baptize* and *wash* are used interchangeably as purely synonymous: "He that baptizeth himself after the touching of a dead body, what availeth his washing?" The allusion is to Numbers xix. 11, etc., where the law simply required washing, or purifying. The essential thing in that purifying was performed by sprinkling; and of him who should fail in this, it was said, "*because the water of separation was not sprinkled upon him*, he shall be unclean; his uncleanness is yet upon him."

If we therefore follow the Scripture pattern, or the pattern of the Greek of the Apocrypha, in fixing the proper idea of the word "baptize" as used to denote the sacred use of water in a religious ordinance, we shall entirely omit all reference to mode, and fix our thoughts upon the intent and the import of baptism; the substance and not the shadow Baptism will not be a dipping, or an immersing, or a pouring, or a sprinkling, but a WASHING, a PURIFYING.

The word being thus used in the New Testament to denote a ritual washing or purifying (which it never signified in classic Greek); being used moreover where the mode of purifying was either sprinkling or pouring; and being, still further, so used that to make it read immerse would make the Bible speak what confessedly is not true; I think we have clearly—and established beyond the possibility of a successful denial—*a generic and peculiar New Testament use of the word; in which use baptize primarily denotes a ritual purifying by some manner of application of water, which is called "the* WASHING *of water:" and secondarily it denotes an inward purifying by the Holy Ghost, called "the* WASHING *of regeneration."*

These things being so, how idle it is for our Baptist brethren to ask, as they often do, "If any application of water, washing, sprinkling, pouring, etc., means baptism, why did not the sacred writers sometimes use the Greek word which means to wash, sprinkle, and pour?"

The reason is plain:

1. Baptize is used with a peculiar but generic reference to this *purifying*, without any reference to mode. But the words "sprinkle" and "pour" are not so used. Their use in the New Testament is

THE SCRIPTURAL IDEA.

not limited to the sacred use of water; and they refer to a *mode;* while the word baptize in the New Testament refers to none. They cannot therefore be interchanged with "baptize" as though they were synonymous with it. The word " wash" *is* so interchanged, because it so far accords with baptize as not to refer to any particular mode.

2. It is not true that the words, wash, sprinkle, pour, are not used in the New Testament *with reference* to baptism. As often as anything is said in the New Testament in allusion to a mode of baptism, these words are invariably used. As to the word *wash,* the Scriptures refer to baptism as the " washing of water;" and the baptism of the Holy Ghost they call " the washing of regeneration." As to the word *sprinkle,* the prophets describe the purifying which they foretell, as a sprinkling: " So shall he sprinkle many nations;" "Then will I sprinkle clean water upon you, and ye shall be clean." As to the word *pour,* the mode of the Spirit's baptizing is spoken of as a pouring, a shedding forth, a falling upon. But where do you read of the *immersing* of (with) " *water,"* or of the *immersing* of many "nations," or of the *immersing* of " regeneration," or of the *immersing* " of (in) the blood of Christ?" Nowhere in the word of God: nowhere, even in figure. The very idea is strange and preposterous. We may retort the question, if it be so, that baptism is nothing but immersion, and that immersion is all essential to it; why is it that we never read of the

11*

immersion of "regeneration"—or of a promise, then I will immerse you in "clean water and ye shall be clean:"—or of the immersion of the blood of Christ?

VII. TRANSLATING THE WORD "BAPTIZE."

Our English translators employed the words *baptize* and *baptism*, which had been for ages in common use, to denote the ordinance, and which had become vernacular in the English tongue. Of Greek origin these words undoubtedly were, but they were as well understood as the words *geography, astronomy, biography, rhetoric, grammar* and *history* are now; which are as truly of Greek original, and as purely Greek, as the words baptize and baptism.

I have proved, as I think, with regard to some passages, that immerse could not have been the sense of baptize, and that the word could not have been so translated consistently with truth. But had such been its meaning, the word immerse could not have been better understood than the word baptize. Immerse is as purely Latin as baptize is Greek. Baptize became an English word as soon as the Gospel was preached in England; and our Baptist brethren contend that baptism was then performed by immersion. Had this been the case, and had the old Britons been taught to consider immersion the essence of baptism, the word baptism in their language would have signified immersion; and the Greek word *baptizo* would have as truly expressed the idea as the Latin word immerse. At all events, as our Baptist brethren claim that the Gospel was first preached in Britain by immersers, and that immersion was the exclusive mode of baptism till near the time our translation was made, they ought for very shame to give over their abuse of our English translators as though they had transferred the word instead of translating it. Either the claims of our Baptist brethren are idle and false, or the transferring was done by immersers; and then their accusations against Pedobaptists, as though they had transferred the word baptize for the purpose of "concealing its true import," are idle and false. Our Baptist brethren may choose which horn of the dilemma they will: either their claims are idle and false, or their accusations are idle and false. The word was, indeed, originally *transferred* into our language: but our English translators did not make the transfer; they gave a proper translation—employing THE VERY word that had been exclusively employed to denote the ordinance, ever since the day that the Christian religion was first planted in their native land. Baptize was then as much an English word as almost any word in the English language, most of the words having been as much derived from a foreign source us the word baptize.

But neither of the words, immerse, sprinkle, pour, nor any other word that relates merely to the *mode* of the ordinance, could express the idea of baptism. Baptism is a sacred rite, of peculiar signification and design. Whatever be the mode of performing it, such a mode of applying water may be a very familiar thing with any people on earth. Such things as dipping, immersing, sprinkling, and pouring, are very common among all nations wherever there is water; and of course every language must have a word for each of these things. But certainly it will not be contended that all heathen nations are in the habit of performing such a thing as a Christian baptism, in the Christian sense. The Baptists do not consider every immersion a *baptism*, in the Christian sense. If they do, then, so far as baptism is concerned, they must hold communion with every man who accidentally falls overboard; if they do not, then they do not consider immersion as equivalent to baptism; and it is idle to pretend that the *word* baptism is equivalent to the *word* immerse, or that immerse is an adequate or faithful translation of the word baptize. On our part we do not hold every man baptized who has been accidentally sprinkled in a shower. We cannot therefore claim that the word baptize is equivalent to the word sprinkle: and do not consider the word sprinkle or the word pour as a proper translation of the word baptize.*

---

* Our Baptist brethren are fond of making a representation touching this matter, which is very plausible and captivating to ignorant and unreflecting minds; but nothing can be more disingenuous in the estimation of those who understand the subject. Thus, Mr. Woolsey, p. 211, endea-

No word which expresses simply a MODE of applying water can fill up the idea of the word *baptizo;* and any word which limits the application to any one mode is an arrant perversion of the Scriptures, which expressly speak of baptism under two modes, sprinkling and pouring; and refer to it again and again under the more general idea of a purifying, or a washing. The mode of immersion is the very one which finds the least countenance in the word of God; if, indeed, there is any unquestionable autho-

---

vors to show what "effort" we make "to get around the plain instruction of the apostle" in Rom. vi. 4, by insinuating that we would have it read,—or take the ground which requires us to read—"Buried with him by *sprinkling.*" The Baptist Bible Society is equally disingenuous and injurious —not only with regard to us, but with regard to the truth in this matter. Thus, in the Appendix to the Report for 1840, p. 52, they say, "If a Pedobaptist translator conscientiously believes that sprinkling or pouring is the meaning of baptizo, let him thus render the word." The reader cannot fail, I think, to see the fallacy and disingenuousness of such an argument, and such a mode of representing Pedobaptist views. Our brethren represent us as holding what I think they must know we do not hold, viz., that baptize in the New Testament signifies a *mode* of applying water; is synonymous with the word sprinkle; and can be adequately and truly translated by the term sprinkle. Assuming that we maintain this, and so representing us, they endeavor to show the absurdity of such ground; and then "covering up and concealing" our real views— *they* endeavor to "*transfer*" that absurdity to our account.

rity for that mode, aside from its being one of the modes of washing or purifying.

In translating the word *baptize*, therefore, we must have a word which possesses two qualities: 1st. It must denote a sacred application of water in a ritual purifying; 2d. It must not limit the application to any one mode. To wash or to purify, comes nearer the true idea, than either of the words, sprinkle or immerse; and they are the only words which can be employed with exclusive reference to a mode of baptizing, consistently with the truth of the Bible. Yet neither *wash*, nor *purify*, has the exact and full signification, by the common acceptation of these terms. To *wash* did not originally, in our language, mean a ritual purification, much less did *immerse* have that meaning; and *to purify* does not in the common use of our language signify necessarily an application of water. We may use them, with a modification of their common meaning; and the connection will show in what sense they are used.

But after all, when the new idea of baptism came into the minds of the old Britons, they needed either a new word, or a new adaptation of an old word to express that idea. They wanted a term which should express *a ritual purifying by some manner of sacred application of water:* and it mattered not what word they employed, nor from what source it was derived, provided they might agree respecting what word should express the idea. To illustrate this,—in the South Sea Islands, they had no knowledge of such a thing as a horse, and of course no word for horse. But in translating the Bible for them, it was necessary to find something to substitute for the word horse. The animal might have been described by a long circumlocution, by the use of words already existing in their language; but this would not do: the word must be translated. How could this be done, as the natives had no word for horse? The Missionaries made a word for them. The Greek word for horse is *Hippos,* and by leaving off the last letter, the word would conform in shape and sound to the structure of native words much better than the English word horse, and quite as well as any other combination of sounds that might be invented. So the Missionaries translated the word horse by the word "*Hippo.*"* But this word would need explanation. Grant it. And so has the

---

* The Missionaries at the Sandwich Islands found the Hawaiian language so copious that they were not under the necessity of introducing a great number of foreign words, except proper names. "We have, however," say they, "adopted Ekalesia for church, bapetiso for baptize, bapetite for baptist, lepero for leper, aeto for eagle, alopeke for fox, bereua for bread, enemi for enemy, himeni for hymn, halelu for psalm, and a few other foreign words, most of which are well established, and familiar to common readers."—[Report of the American Bible Society, 1837.] The classical and Biblical scholar will at once recognize the origin of these words.

word *baptizo* to be explained by Baptist translators, and they explain it to mean—most erroneously as we believe—immersion.

NO NEW THING TO TRANSFER PECULIAR WORDS FROM ONE LANGUAGE TO ANOTHER.

This transferring of words from one language to another is not so uncommon a process as many of our brethren seem to suppose it. What English word shall be substituted for the Greek word "Tetrarch," in Luke iii. 1? What for the Greek word "Pentecost," in Acts ii. 1? What for the Greek words "Christ" and "Christians?" "Christ" signifies *anointed;* and so does the Hebrew "Messiah." But to *translate* the word, in all cases, on the principle contended for by our Baptist brethren, would confound and destroy the meaning of many passages of Scripture. The word is applied by way of eminence, as an appellation, to the promised Redeemer. In Matt. i. 1, 18, and Mark i., as often elsewhere, our Lord is called, not "Jesus, the Christ," but "Jesus Christ." As George Campbell well says (D. V., Part 4), "Though the word *Anointed* expresses the primitive import of the Hebrew name, it does not convey the idea in which it was then universally understood. It was considered solely as the well known title of an extraordinary office, to which there was nothing similar among the people." That the word *Christ* has this peculiar meaning when applied to the Saviour, may be seen at once, by applying the word, in its English sense, to other personages, who are often spoken of by the same original words, both in Hebrew and Greek. How would it sound to hear David speaking of Saul, as in Sam. xxiv. 6, repeatedly call that wicked king the "Christ of the Lord?" How would it sound in Isa. xlv. 1, to hear the Lord speaking to Cyrus, as to his "Christ?" or, in Psalm cv., "Touch not my Christs?" Here the sense as imperatively demands that the word be translated according to its original import, as other passages do that it should not be translated but *transferred*.

I suppose it would be lawful to talk to the Hindoos, or the Burmans, about the Jewish "Synagogues," though that too is a word of Greek origin. If any heathen have no term for such beings as devils, I suppose it would be lawful to introduce to them such words as the Greek *Diabolos*, or the English word *devil*. It would be a matter of indifference whether you introduce to them our Hebraic English word "*Sabbath*," and teach them its meaning; or teach them how to use one of their own old words with a new meaning. The volume of God's word might retain its Greek-English name *Bible*, or it might be turned into the words vernacular among the heathen, for "writings," or for "The Book;" only teaching them to give a new idea to their common words. Such words as "Jubilee," "homer," "epah," "shekel," "cherubim," might be transferred, or old words selected, and taught to bear a meaning not originally their own, as should be found most convenient.

A scholar, dealing in profane literature only, in translating from the ancient Greek writers, or from Cicero or Tacitus, might find himself compelled, either to give erroneous ideas, or to transfer into Burmese, or Japanese, such words as "Archon," "Consul," "Prætor," "Questor," "Censor," "Senator," "Dictator," "Tribune." "Who," says Campbell, "considers these names" (as transferred into our language) "as barbarous?" "To have employed instead of them 'Alderman,' 'Sheriff,' etc., we should have justly thought much more exceptionable." "I have heard," says he, "of a Dutch translator of Cæsar's Commentaries, who always rendered "consul" *burgomaster;* and in the same taste, all the other officers and magistrates of Rome." How could we have translated the Latin classics, and given the true idea, unless we had naturalized, in such cases, the very Latin words, and learned the ideas and the names together? Where would have been our English ideas of such a thing as a "libation," an "ovation," a "lustration," had we not imported, not only the names, but the very ideas, from the language and customs of heathenism? Whence comes our English word "triumph?" Whence come the now English words "Sultan," "Pacha," "Khan," "Bey?" What limit is there to the transferring of the very words of the people who bring us new things and new ideas? Look at our military terms: almost all adopted and transferred from the French. Look at our terms of chemistry, botany, and zoology: how many of them have been recently compounded from the Greek?

Now, unless baptism is already in use among the heathen, as a RELIGIOUS PURIFICATION, and expressed by a word of their own, having this precise idea, in distinction from the idea of any simple *mode* of administering water, or at least in *addition* to such an idea of mode, it must be as inadequate and inaccurate a translation which shall use an old word of theirs, referring simply to the *mode* of applying water, as it would be to turn the Roman "Consul" into a Dutch "Burgomaster." The translation is inadequate; it is incorrect; it misleads; and that aside from the consideration that to translate *Baptize, immerse,* makes the Bible speak falsehood, even with regard to the mere mode. You may transfer the word *Baptize;* you may call baptism in Siamese (as the Baptist Bible Society say our missionaries have done), "*Bapteetsamay,*" conforming the shape of the word to the genius of the language, as in the Latin *Baptizare,* and the English *baptize;* and it is correct. It is as easy to teach them the new word as it is to teach them the new idea—the positive and peculiar Scripture idea of baptize. Or you may translate baptize into a word signifying to WASH; still better, if you can find a word which signifies a ritual purifying by washing; and you have given a most faithful translation. But to translate the word by the word *immerse*, is to give an inadequate, inaccurate, and, as we contend, a false idea.

MARTIN LUTHER'S VERSION.

Our Baptist brethren claim that Luther translated baptize by the word *dip* or *immerse*. Thus:

Mr. Woolsey says, p. 74, " Luther, one of the great reformers, gave the Bible translated to the Germans, that they might read in their own language the wonderful works of God; and he rendered baptize into a word signifying to immerse." Again he says, p. 138, " Or as Luther, the great reformer, renders it in his German Testament," *Johannes der Taufer*,—" John the Dipper."

So the Baptist Bible Society, in their report for 1840, p. 89, say, " Other translators may do as they please; baptize may be twisted into all sorts of meanings except immersion—unless, indeed, in the case of old versions. Luther may say that it means to immerse, and his version shall continue to be circulated; but wo be to the Baptists if *they* say so; and what is the reason?"

Mr. Woolsey compliments Luther, as "this bold defender of the inalienable rights of every man to become personally acquainted with the truths of the Bible faithfully translated into his own vernacular tongue."

We all agree with Mr. Woolsey in venerating the courage, the honesty, and the piety of Martin Luther. But is Mr. Woolsey ignorant that the Germans, and all Lutherans who use his translation, baptize by sprinkling, as Luther practiced and as Luther taught them? When a German minister takes water in his hand and *sprinkles* or *pours* it on the person baptized, saying, "ICH TAUFE DICH," does he mean *I immerse you?* Do the people so understand him? Most certainly not. When Martin Luther took water in his hand, and poured or sprinkled it on the head of a person, saying, "*Ich taufe dich*," did he mean "I immerse you?" Would the people so understand him? It is impossible. Luther could never have used that word in connection with such an action, had it in his day been equivalent to immerse. The words *Taufen* and *Taufer*, which Mr. Woolsey and the Baptist Bible Society translate "immerse" and "dipper," mean no such thing. They are used in German with specific and exclusive reference to the rite of baptism, which the Germans perform by sprinkling or affusion.

Thus, the English and German Dictionary, by E. A. Weber, of acknowledged and unquestionable authority, gives the following definitions of the words in question. I copy from the Leipsic edition of 1833, by Tauchnitz:

Taufe, baptism, christening.
Taufen, to baptize, to christen.
Taufer, baptizer, baptist.

Taufling, person baptized.
Taufname, Christian name.
Taufclein, certificate from the church register.

The same dictionary gives the following German words for the English words, immerge, immerse and immersion. It will be seen that *Taufen* is not among them.

Immerge, eintauchen, versunken, vertiefen.
Immerse, eintauchen, untertauchen, vertiefen.
Immersion, untertauchung, versunkung.

Burckhardt, in his German and English Lexicon (ed. Berlin, 1823), gives the same definitions, both in the English and in the German.

From this it is manifest, that whatever might have been the etymology of the words *Taufen* and *Taufer,* they do not in German mean *immerse* or *immerser.* To give a German an idea of immersion you must use other words, different both in their origin, their meaning, and their form.

The world will doubtless concur with Mr. Woolsey in his encomium upon Luther as "this bold defender of the inalienable right of every man" to have the Bible "faithfully translated into his vernacular tongue." Doubtless Luther meant to give "the Bible translated to the Germans, that they might read in their own language the wonderful works of God." But the reader may judge whether Mr. Woolsey would not have spared his encomium upon Luther, had he not, in talking about Luther's translation, undertaken to talk about a matter concerning which he was not well informed. Because our English translators render the word baptize by the word wash in Mark vii. 4, and Luke xi. 38, Mr. Woolsey declares that they have been guilty of a "glaring perversion of this Scripture, by suppressing the word *baptize*, and substituting the word *wash*," p. 152. He contends, p. 153, that "the translators of our English Bible, for the sake of suppressing the true import of the words baptize and baptism," "have not only concealed" the "instructions of the Holy Ghost," but "represented the Holy Ghost as using the most stupid tautology." But how does that "great reformer," and "bold defender," translate these passages? Mr. Woolsey declares that *he* has given to the Germans a Bible *translated*. How does Luther translate these passages? He translates them by the word "WASH," the pure old Saxon word, the identical mother of our good old English word "*wash*." "*Und wenn sie vom Markte kommen, essen sie nicht, sie* WASCHEN SICH *denn;*"—they WASH THEMSELVES. So in Luke xi. 38, "*Da das der Pharisaer sah verwunderte* er sich, dass er sich nicht vor dem essen GEWASCHEN HATTE,"—that he *had not* WASHED *himself*."

THE PESHITO-SYRIAC VERSION.

Our baptist brethren claim this version as evidence in favor of immersion. Thus, Mr. Woolsey affirms, p. 71, that "the venerable Peshito-Syriac version," which he thinks was "evidently executed by the last of the first century," has *baptize* translated by *immerse*.

If this were so, I think we have shown from higher authority, even from the Scriptures themselves, that such a translation is wrong. The testimony of Evangelists and Apostles is as good against the mere opinion of all translators, as it is against testimony adduced from the heathen Greeks.

But will Mr. Woolsey admit this translation to be good authority on the subject of baptism? Will Mr. Woolsey, after affirming, p. 252, that "not a word is said about Infant Baptism," "till the *third* century;" will he, after all that he has said about "Mistress Lydia," p. 305, and its being "quite certain that she was a maiden lady," p. 306; will Mr. Woolsey, after this, admit the "venerable Peshito-Syriac version," this "Protoplastic version," "the very best that has ever been made," as good authority on the subject of baptism? This Syriac version reads, that "when she (Lydia) was baptized WITH HER CHILDREN."* Will Mr. Woolsey, after affirming that this version was made by the last of the first century, and maintaining that it "cannot be determined" whether "it be the work of an inspired apostle or not," will he now admit that he was wrong in declaring so positively that there is nowhere any mention of Infant Baptism till the *third century?*

---

* Kurtz, p. 99. The Coptic version gives the same reading.

Will he admit, that he and all the Baptists are wrong in denying that Infant Baptism existed before the close of the second century, and acknowledge that the practice can be traced clearly and indubitably to the apostles : or will he for ever after be silent about the "immersion" of the venerable "Peshito-Syriac version ?"

But it is not admitted that the Syriac version renders the word baptize by a word signifying immerse. The best scholars deny it. Professor Stuart shows that while the Syriac has a word, which means to plunge, dip, or immerse, the Syriac version does not employ that word, but another, which signifies "to confirm—to establish," so that "Baptism, then, in the language of the Peshito, is the *rite of confirmation* simply, while the manner of this is apparently left without being at all expressed."* An English Baptist, who is, as says a competent judge, "evidently a master in Israel," has recently written against the "Baptist Translation Society. This writer accords with Professor Stuart with regard to the meaning of the Syraic word by which baptize is translated in the version in question." "I confess," says he, "I can derive no countenance to my practice as a Baptist from this version." Concerning the Ethiopic and Coptic versions, he admits that "they must be set aside, if they are not used

---

* From Judd's Reply to Professor Stuart, p. 164.

against us (the Baptists) in the baptismal controversy."*

The ancient Syriac version is the present Bible of the Nestorian Christians. Their modern word for baptize is radically the word employed in the ancient version, and like the German *taufen*, and the English *baptize*, it is exclusively appropriated to the ordinance of baptism. They baptize either by immersion or affusion, and make no objection when they see our missionaries baptize by sprinkling, but consider it as good and valid baptism. Mr. Woolsey is, therefore, as much mistaken here, as he is in the case of Martin Luther's version.

DUTCH, DANISH AND SWEDISH VERSIONS.

Our Baptist brethren affirm, that the "Dutch, Danish and Swedish versions have the words in dispute translated by words signifying immersion."†

On this subject I will simply quote the words of Dr. Henderson, who has studied the languages of Northern Europe on the ground, and is familiar with their idioms. Dr. Henderson is authority upon this subject, which will not probably be questioned.

---

* See New York Evangelist, Jan. 23, 1841.

† Report of the American Foreign Bible Society, 1840, p. 88. Woolsey, p. 188.

Says Dr. Henderson, "As it respects the Gothic dialects, which have been repeatedly appealed to with great confidence, it is a settled point with all who are acquainted with them, that the reference is totally irrelevant. That the Maeso-Gothic *daupian*, the Anglo-Saxon *dyppan*, the Dutch *doopen*, the Swedish *dopa*, the Danish *dobe*, and the German *taufen*, all correspond in sound to our English word *dip*, does not admit of any dispute, any more than the fact that *dab*, *daub* and *dub* have the same correspondence; but nothing would be more erroneous than to conclude, with the exception of the Anglo-Saxon, that they must have the same signification. No Dutchman, Dane, Swede or German would for a moment imagine that the words belonging to their respective languages meant anything else than baptism, by the application of water to the body baptized. The words are never used in those languages in another sense, or in application to any other subject. Where the Germans would express *dip* or *immerse*, they employ *tauchen* and not *taufen*, which is the word by which *baptize* is translated. The Danes, in like manner, use *dyppe* and *neddyppe*, for *dip*, and not *dobe*. And that neither Luther, nor the authors of the Dutch, Danish and Swedish versions, had any intention of conveying the idea of immersion as implied in baptize, is obvious from the preposition which they have used with the verb. Thus we read in German, *mit* wasser taufen; in Danish, dobe *met* vand; in Swedish, dopa *med* vatn;

in Dutch, doopen *met* wasser; *i. e.*, *with* water, and not *in* wasser—*in* water, *i* vand, *i* vatn; which phraseology is as foreign to these languages as the practice which it would sanction is unknown to the inhabitants of the countries in which they are spoken. Even the Mennonites in Holland, and other parts, though they reject Infant Baptism, administer the ordinance by pouring, and not by immersion."

THE VULGATE.

Our Baptist brethren are equally hostile to the Vulgate as to the English version for having transferred the word baptize. Thus, Mr. Woolsey says, p. 82, that "The Roman Catholic Bible, *i. e.*, the Latin Vulgate, was the first to transfer baptize and other words, rather than translate them." Again, p. 83, he calls the Vulgate the "authorized Roman Bible." On p. 89, he classes our English Bible and the Vulgate together as "unworthy models."

Now it is true that the Vulgate is the "authorized Bible" in the Roman Catholic church. But it is also true that the Vulgate was made before the Papal church had an existence. The Vulgate was declared the standard version of the Roman church by the Council of Trent, 1545: but it ought not to be forgotten that it was to an old copy of the Vulgate, which providentially fell into the hands of Martin Luther, long before the Council of Trent, that we owe the Reformation. The Bible on which the Reformation was built, and which was in use by all the Western churches, before the Papal church was born, ought not, surely, thus to be thrown by with a sarcasm, as "The Roman Catholic Bible." In the time of Jerome, who was born about A. D. 330, there were several Latin versions of the Bible and of parts of the Bible. One of them, adopted by ecclesiastical authority, had long been called the Vulgate, or common version. In the process of transcribing many times, many mistakes had crept into the common copies. In A. D. 383, Jerome began a revision of this ancient *Vulgata*, or *Itala* version— having before him the original Hebrew of the Old Testament, the original Greek of the New, together with the Hexapla of Origen. With these, and with all other aids before him which the age afforded, Jerome sat down to the revision of the old Itala, or Vulgate; a part of which revision is still extant (the book of Job, and the book of Psalms), the remainder is lost. But impressed with the necessity of a new version, and counselled by friends, he began at the same time a new version, which he completed A. D. 405, and which is now the well known Vulgate. This gradually prevailed, and in time entirely supplanted the old Itala.

In this version the Greek, *baptize*, is adopted into the Latin as a Latin word. It was probably so in the old Itala. Jerome could not have changed the practice of the whole Latin church in administering the ordinance of baptism, and taught them to say *"baptizo te,"* instead of *"submergo* te," had the latter or any such word been in common use. I see no reason to doubt that, from the very day that baptism was first administered at Rome, or in the Latin tongue, the word *baptize* was at once adopted into the Latin tongue by a transfer from the Greek; and if so, it was done either by, or with the sanction of the Apostles themselves. At all events, while there was a common Latin word for *immerse* and for *submerge* (these two English words are taken from the Latin)—Jerome, and the Christian world with him, did not employ either *submergo* or *immergo*, but *baptizo*. Now the Baptists affirm that the whole Christian world were Baptists at that time; *i. e.*, that they considered baptism to be synonymous with immersion, and practiced accordingly. If this were so, then the Vulgate is rather a Baptist Bible than a Roman Catholic Bible; and immersers first led the way in transferring the word baptize, instead of translating it by a word in common use. This outcry about "transferring" and "concealing" comes to this at last.

But an argument may be built upon these facts. The ancient Western church, whose common language was Latin, had an abundant supply of words to express *immersion* and *submersion*, if they had thought immersion the only baptism, or essential to it. But so far from employing one of their common words, they transferred the original Greek word *baptize*, adopted it into their language, and gave it a complete naturalization. When they spoke of baptism, they called it an ablution, a washing, a distilling of the purifying dew: they spoke of it not as an immersion. As to the manner of performing baptism, even when they generally practiced immersion, they did not always do so, and of course never deemed it essential. What is the inevitable conclusion from these facts? That they did not consider the word immerse, or the word submerge, as equivalent to the word baptize; and that a substitution of these words for that would not be an adequate or faithful translation.

Here, then, we have the judgment of the ancient church with regard to the propriety of transferring the word in question; and that judgment founded upon the conviction that neither of their existing words would truly and adequately express the true idea of Christian baptism.

This was the judgment of the Christian church in the time of Jerome; and in his days the use of baptizo, as a common Latin word, was a custom, whereof the memory of man ran not to the contrary —as a practice in which all Christians who spoke the Latin language acquiesced and undoubtingly agreed. The TRANSFER was, without any ground for doubt of which I am informed, MADE IN THE DAYS OF THE APOSTLES THEMSELVES. It is not, as Mr.

Woolsey's book and the Report of the Baptist Bible Society would lead those to suppose who are not otherwise informed, a recent invention, to oppose the Baptists, and "to conceal a part of God's revealed will from the nations of the earth, in a dead language, with a view of promoting party designs, and of preventing men from knowing his will, and their duty and obligation to obey him."

IV.

INFANT BAPTISM.

SCRIPTURAL AUTHORITY.

There are two questions with regard to baptism, on which evangelical Christians are divided; one respecting the *mode*, and the other respecting the *subjects*. These two questions are entirely distinct, and there is no reason why those who differ concerning one might not agree concerning the other.

Between us and our Baptist brethren there is no difference of opinion concerning the subjects of baptism, except concerning infants. We agree that adults are not to be baptized, save on a credible profession of evangelical faith and repentance. The questions concerning the subjects are therefore limited to this single inquiry: *Are the infant children of believing parents to be baptized?*

The law of the institution makes no express mention of infants. It is therefore contended that this is conclusive against Infant Baptism; as in a positive institution we are to go by the letter of the law; and all beyond this, as well as everything short of this, is wrong.

I humbly conceive, however, that Christ has a right to make known his will, in this or in any other matter, in just such a way as he pleases; that the incidental recognition, by the Apostles, of infants, as properly embraced in the intent of that law, or their actual practice of baptizing infants, would be an authoritative interpretation of the law, as extending its provisions to infants. And we deceive ourselves; we undertake to correct the wisdom of our Lord Jesus Christ; we are guilty of disobedience to his authority; if, in such a case, we allow any notions or arguments about a "positive institution" to lead us to act in opposition to the will of Christ, no less truly made known than if the warrant had expressed infants by name. The question is not, *Are infants expressly named;* but, *Has Christ anywhere, and in any way, instructed us whether they are to be embraced or excluded?*

On this principle our Baptist brethren themselves argue and practice in other matters; and that, too, in matters pertaining to "positive institutions." Indeed, any other principle than this would shut out the Lord Jesus Christ from being master and lawgiver over his own house. Who are we, to prescribe to him how he is to make known his will; and that under penalty of having his will rejected, if he does not make it known in just the manner that we think he ought to employ?

The *Sabbath* is a positive institution; ard God has expressly designated the seventh day; yet all

Christians in the world, who keep a Sabbath, save a very diminutive fraction of one sect, keep the first day. Where is the express warrant for this change? There is none. Our Baptist brethren, like ourselves, make out a warrant by inference. We find the will of Christ made known in the Scriptures,—not expressly, but circumstantially. The practice of the Apostles teaches the will of Christ, even though it be but incidentally mentioned. We admit the validity of this warrant by inference. If truly made out, it is as clearly the will of Christ as though we had found an express warrant in so many words, "Let the Sabbath be changed from the seventh day to the first."

The "Seventh Day Baptists" are the only consistent ones here. They do with the Sabbath as they do by Infant Baptism; they admit nothing but an express warrant, in so many words, to bear upon either question; "and," said one of their ministers to me, "we feel that with our Baptist brethren our arguments are unanswerable. *They must either keep the seventh day as the Sabbath, or else reject the very principles on which they reject Infant Baptism; they must give up their argument, or keep the seventh day, or else determine to act inconsistently and absurdly.*"

His conclusion was manifestly sound. And I could not help adding, both you and they must give up *female communion*, too; for when Christ instituted his Supper, there were no female disciples present, though he had such at the time, and he said not one word about them in the law of the ordinance; nor are they anywhere expressly mentioned as partaking in the celebration of the ordinance; and yet the Lord's Supper is purely a "positive institution," and, say our brethren, you must go by the letter; you must not go beyond; you must not make out a warrant by inference; you must have it express.

I know they prove the propriety of female communion; but they prove it by INFERENCE, and not by any EXPRESS command or precept. I admit the proof to be valid; but neither our Baptist brethren nor anybody else can make it out, without at the same time sweeping away the very foundation of their argument against Infant Baptism.

I only insist that the same sort of proof be considered equally valid to prove the authority for Infant Baptism. I am willing to have it required that that proof be ample. I have no fear for the issue, if the condition of receiving Infant Baptism be ten times the amount of proof required to substantiate the change of the Sabbath, or to make out the Scriptural warrant for female communion.

You perceive that I have here made a "concession;" if it be proper to call that a concession, which concerns a thing that we never attempted to hold, and which is a simple statement of a truth that every Pedobaptist in the world was always free to acknowledge. The "concession" is, that the law of baptism makes no EXPRESS mention of infants.

But having made this concession, I must be allowed to enter my protest against being understood or reported to have conceded that the Scriptures furnish no warrant for Infant Baptism. I concede no such thing. I maintain the contrary. Nor will it be deemed a matter of wonder to those who know what use is sometimes made of concessions, that I should deem it necessary to enter this protest.

Thus, a concession of Dr. Woods is sometimes quoted in such a way as to leave those who hear it under the impression, that Dr. Woods admits that the Scriptures furnish no warrant for Infant Baptism.* So far as his words are quoted, they are quoted correctly from p. 11 of his work on Infant Baptism: "Whatever may have been the precepts of Christ or his apostles to those who enjoyed their personal instructions, it is a plain case that there is no express precept respecting Infant Baptism in our sacred writings."

Here the matter is left. The quotation is truth as far as it goes; but what is essential to the truth is omitted, and the omission causes Dr. Woods to be understood as giving up all claim of a Scriptural warrant for Infant Baptism; whereas, in truth, Dr. Woods gives his testimony directly to the contrary.

---

* The writer has himself heard Dr. Woods quoted in this manner before a full congregation.

His "concession" refers only to an "express precept." His work was written for the very purpose of proving the Scriptural warrant for Infant Baptism. He is very explicit (p. 42), to take his position in the most formal words, and he prints them in italics that this position may be well noted and understood: and these are his words:

"But I shall now proceed to argue the point from the INSPIRED RECORDS just as they are. *My position is, that the Scriptures of the New Testament, understood according to the just rules of interpretation,* IMPLY THAT THE CHILDREN OF BELIEVERS ARE TO BE BAPTIZED."

In the same manner, in a tract published by the "General Baptist Tract Society," entitled, "THE SCRIPTURE GUIDE TO BAPTISM, by Pengilly," and widely circulated both here and elsewhere, Richard Baxter is introduced as speaking in the strongest terms against Infant Baptism. One long quotation from his writings introduced for this purpose, ends with these words: "I profess my conscience is fully satisfied from this text, that it is one sort of faith, even saving, THAT MUST GO BEFORE BAPTISM." The last words are printed in capitals. Jewett, in his work on Baptism, has introduced the same quotation for the same purpose, to make Richard Baxter bear his witness against Infant Baptism.

And again, "*The Scripture Guide to Baptism, by Pengilly,*" (p. 44), after asserting in italics, "*that we have nowhere found a single place or passage that describes, records, or implies the baptism of any infants;*" says, "the reader will not suppose this a hasty conclusion when he hears the following Pedobaptists." Under this, he again quotes Baxter thus: "I conclude that all examples of baptism in Scripture do mention only the administration of it to the professors of saving faith; and the precepts give us no other direction. And I provoke Mr. Blake, as far as is seemly for me to do, to name one precept or example for any other, and make it good if he can."

Here is a point in question, and witnesses are called. Richard Baxter is brought upon the stand *Mr. Baxter, Is Infant Baptism right according to the word of God?* An answer is put into his mouth, taken from his works, in which he is reasoning—not concerning infants—but concerning adults; and showing that "it is one sort of faith, even saving" (and not simply the intellectual belief of an unconverted man), "that must go before baptism." And so, Richard Baxter is by this process made to bear witness against Infant Baptism!

But, Mr. Baxter, you were a Pedobaptist; did you not baptize children, and so teach and exhort in the house of God? O yes, and dearly prized the ordinance, and would not have given it up sooner than I would have given up my life. But, Mr. Baxter, what is this then that they say of you? Your name is spread abroad in tracts upon tracts, and in books upon books, and goes out to the four winds of heaven;

and your own strong language is printed in the boldest relief, as though the author of the "Saint's Rest," and of the "Call to the Unconverted," had borne his testimony most decidedly against Infant Baptism! Are you so opposed, Mr. Baxter? Is this witness true of you? What say you of Infants, Mr. Baxter? Do you cut these off from the Church of God?

To be so quoted is well nigh enough to call the dead "Saint" from his "Rest." He answers on this point, and it is Baxter's own strong emotion and burning words that speak: "GOD," says Mr. Baxter, "GOD HAD NEVER A CHURCH ON EARTH, OF WHICH INFANTS WERE NOT INFANT MEMBERS, SINCE THERE WERE INFANTS IN THE WORLD."*

---

* Baxter's Comment. on Matt. xxviii. 19 (in GRAY on the Authority for Infant Baptism, Halifax, 1837, p. 200).

The hottest controversy which Mr. Baxter ever had was with the Baptists. A Mr. Tombes had written a book against Infant Baptism, and thought that Baxter was "the chief hinderer" of its success: "Though," says Mr. Baxter, "I never meddled with that point." "He had," says Baxter, "so high a conceit of his writings that he thought them unanswerable, and that none could deal with them in that way." "At last, somehow, he urged me to give my judgment of them; when I let him know they did not satisfy me to be of his mind, but went no further with him." "But he unavoidably contrived to bring me into the controversy which I shunned." In the end Baxter agreed to hold a public discussion in Mr. Tombes' church, Jan. 1, 1649. "This dispute," says Baxter, "satisfied all my own people, and the country that came in, and Mr. Tombes' own townsmen, ex-

But enough of these "concessions." Enough of these clouds of quotations from Pedobaptist writers to make them say what, quoted in such connections and for such purposes, is heaven-wide from the faith in which they lived and in which they died. What is done to Woods and to Baxter is done to Calvin, and to a host of others. These men went to the word of God for their doctrine. Whatever would not stand by that rule, they scrupulously rejected with loathing and abhorrence, "hating even the garment spotted by the flesh." They taught and practiced sprinkling and pouring for baptism; they taught and practiced the baptism of infants; for the warrant of both they went to the word of God. And

---

cept about twenty whom he had perverted, who gathered into his church; which never increased to above twenty-two that I could learn."

Not long after, Baxter published his work, entitled, "PLAIN SCRIPTURE PROOF OF INFANTS' CHURCH MEMBERSHIP AND BAPTISM." This work passed through several editions. "The book," says Baxter, "God blessed with unexpected success to stop abundance from turning Anabaptists, and reclaiming many."

Nineteen years after, Baxter published another work, entitled, "MORE PROOFS OF INFANT CHURCH MEMBERSHIP, AND CONSEQUENTLY THEIR RIGHTS TO BAPTISM." This book is divided into three parts, which contain, he tells us, "The plain proof of God's statute or covenant for Infants' church membership from the creation, and the continuance of it till the institution of Baptism; with the defence of that proof against the frivolous exceptions of Mr. Tombes."—(*Ormes' Life and Times of Baxter*, Vol. ii., p. 252.)

now, the influence of their names and the weight of their piety is attempted to be laid into the scale against the doctrines which they practiced and taught, as the truth and the ordinances of God. Is this dealing kindly and truly with the dead? Is this dealing kindly and righteously with the truth?

In the same manner, in this work by Pengilly, published by the Baptist General Tract Society as the "Scripture Guide to Baptism," the names of such men as Doddridge, Baxter, Erskine, Matthew Henry, Calvin, Saurin, Guyse, Charnock, are arrayed as if against us in the particulars in which we differ from our Baptist brethren. Take the names from the book and the quotations annexed to them, and the book is left a mere lifeless carcase. But hear them fully, hear them truly, and do they stand against us? Could they come up from the dead into the midst of this community, to a man they would wend their way to these walls for the truth and order which they held as established by the word of God. To a man they would lift up their voices for the ordinances which now their names are made to impugn. They would cry out upon the injustice done to their memories and to the truth, by these attempts to cast the weight of their names against what they taught and practiced, as the truth and the ordinances of God.

And others, whose names are quoted in this tract by Pengilly, though they might not in all respects agree with us, would nevertheless give us their united voice on the matter now in question. The Methodists, Whitefield and Wesley; the Episcopal, Scott; the Bishops of the Church of England, Tillotson, Burnet, and Taylor, and Archbishop Secker, would cry out upon the injustice done to their names in arraying them, as if witnesses, against the truth and the ordinances which they held as most assuredly the truth and the ordinances of God.

But turn from the authority of names to the foundations on which these men rested their faith. "To the law, and to the testimony."

In our examination of the circumstances which bear upon the interpretation of the Law of Baptism, it will appear:

I. *That the Abrahamic and the Christian Church are one and the same; built on the same covenant; saved with the same faith; and considered in the word of God as one and the same Church.*

II. *That circumcision and baptism are alike seals of the same covenant, and signs of the same thing.*

III. *That the children of believers, as they were connected with the Abrahamic Church, are recognized in the New Testament as sustaining the same relation to the Christian Church.*

If these things can be proved by the certain warrant of the word of God, it will follow that the law of Baptism in the Christian Church is to be interpreted as extending to the children of believing parents. It would seem useless to deny the sign to them who have the thing; and as the seal was once expressly extended to children, if they are to be excepted afterwards, in the application of another sign, of the same meaning, intent and use, the exception must be specified, otherwise the sign follows with the thing. God having given his charter, and sealed it to a specified class of persons, afterwards while he expressly continues the charter, but changes the form of the seal, the seal in that changed form remains of course. Without an express warrant from God, man may not take away the charter, or refuse the seal.

If, in addition to this, we find:

IV. Grounds for concluding that the Apostles applied the sign; and certain history to show that the whole church received the practice, as they believed, from the Apostles; and so practised, uniformly, all over the world, with not a man to raise his voice against the divine authority of the practice for more than thirty generations after Christ; I think we may rest the question as settled. It is not only lawful, but a correct and authorized interpretation of the law of the institution requires believing parents to cause their infant children to be baptized.

This is the outline of the argument which I shall pursue. And now to the proof.

I. *The Abrahamic and the Christian Church are one and the same.*

The Lord appeared to Abraham (Gen. xii. 1–3), and promised that in him should "all the families of the earth be blessed." In Gen. xvii 1–14, God again promised that Abraham should be "the father of many nations;" and that he would be "a God to him and to his seed after him." At the same time God gave him the ordinance of circumcision for himself and for his seed.

Here was the commencement of the polity of the peculiar people of God intended by the term CHURCH; and distinguished (Rom. iii. 2) as having entrusted to them "the oracles of God;" and (Rom. ix. 5) as those to whom "pertain the adoption, and the covenants, and the service of God, and the promises;" and declared (1 Tim. iii. 15) to be "the house of God;" "the church of the living God;" "the pillar and ground of the truth."

On account of this covenant, God is called the "God of Abraham, and of Isaac, and of Jacob;" rather than the God of Enoch, or of Noah, or of Moses, or of David. He is called THEIR GOD in relation to this covenant; as in numberless instances, so particularly in 2 Cor. vi. 16, as God hath said, "I will dwell in them and walk in them; and I will be their God, and they shall be my people;" *i. e.*, their God, as he is not the God of other men; and they his people, as other men are not his people. So in Heb. xi. 16, "Wherefore God is not ashamed to be called THEIR GOD."

This people of God, as an external visible polity, is called "Israel" or the "Church;" as in Acts vii. 38. the descendants of Jacob are called "the Church in the wilderness;" just as the visible polity of Christ's people are called "the Church;" as in 1 Cor. xii. 28, "And God hath set some in the Church; first apostles; secondarily prophets; thirdly teachers," etc. Here the word Church does not mean simply an "assembly;" for it is no particular assembly that is here spoken of, but Christ's visible people everywhere; his Church in the widest sense.

But the visible Church is never made up exclusively of those who shall be saved; and so the terms "Israel" and "Church" are used ordinarily to designate the body of those who are apparently his; to wit, the visible polity made up of good and bad. Again, they are sometimes used to denote particularly those only who shall be the heirs of salvation. Thus, the first term is used in both senses in the following passage, Rom. ix. 6, "For they are not all Israel which are of Israel." And the "kingdom of God" (the visible Church) is represented, Matt. xiii. 47, as a "net cast into the sea, which gathered of every kind;" though cast only for the proper kinds. When full and drawn to the shore, the good are gathered in vessels; the bad are thrown away.

Now *the covenant* on which the Abrahamic Church was founded, was not a covenant of works, but of grace; and its promise was not simply of the land of Canaan, but of Heaven. Thus, Rom. iv. 13, "For the promise that he should be heir of the world, was not to Abraham or to his seed through the law, but through the righteousness of faith." And (ver. 12) "He received the sign of circumcision, a seal of the righteousness of faith which he had, being yet uncircumcised."

It has been strenuously asserted that the covenant was one of temporal promises only, and circumcision given as a mere national badge (and indeed it is necessary for those who reject Infant Baptism to say something of the kind). But the word of God teaches us otherwise. "Abraham was justified by faith." Rom. iv. 13, "The promise was ... through the righteousness of faith ;" and circumcision was "a seal of the righteousness of faith ;" to wit, of the "faith by which men must be justified." So we are taught expressly (Heb. xi.) that Abraham, and Isaac, and Jacob, and Sara, and "multitudes" of their descendants, as the sand which is by the sea shore innumerable, "died in the faith ;" not simply in faith of the promise of Canaan, but of Heaven. Thus, Heb. xi. 13, 15, "And confessed that they were strangers and pilgrims on the earth,"—"but now they desire a better country, that is a Heavenly :" wherefore God is not ashamed to be called their God; "for he hath prepared for them a city." What "city," but *Heaven?*

And since there is no other name than Christ whereby man must be saved, Acts iv. 12, since there is "one God and one mediator between God and man," 1 Tim. ii. 5, these men *believed on Christ.* This we are expressly taught. Thus, "Abraham rejoiced to see my day, and he saw it, and was glad." So of all the ancient Israelites who were saved it is expressly said, 1 Cor. x. 2–4, "And were all baptized unto Moses in the cloud and in the sea; and did all eat of the same spiritual meat; and did all drink of the same spiritual drink: for they drank of that spiritual rock that followed them; and that rock was Christ."

Here pause a moment. Was not that the true Church, whose true members

Believed on Christ;

Sought a Heavenly country;

Were justified by faith;

Of whom the world was not worthy;

For whom God prepared a city;

And who are now set down in the kingdom of God?

In what respect does the Church of Christ differ from this, in the articles which may well be judged the Articles of the true Church of God?

"But the Jewish polity is passed away." True. But the Abrahamic Church is quite a different thing from the Jewish polity. Thus, Gal. iii. 17, "And this I say, that the *covenant*, that was confirmed before of God in Christ, the law, which was four hundred and thirty years after, cannot disannul, that it should make the promise of none effect." And if the giving of the law did not annul the covenant, certainly the covenant is not annulled by the removing of the ceremonial law. And this is the very thing for which Paul is arguing; and which the Holy Ghost, who inspired him, teaches through his arguments—that the covenant and its blessings remain, and come upon the Gentiles, as Paul says in express words (v. 11), "That the blessing of Abraham might come on the Gentiles through Jesus Christ."

Now "Circumcision was not of Moses but of the fathers," John vii. 22. It was the seal of a covenant which existed before the law; and neither the giving of the law, nor the removal of it, affected either the covenant or the seal. The covenant remaining, the seal remained, of course, unless specially abrogated. Another form of the seal was indeed adopted under Christ, as another day was adopted for the Sabbath, instead of the seventh.

The seal being changed, circumcision was interdicted (Acts xv.), but this was especially on the ground that those who enjoined circumcision, taught that it was needful to circumcise them and "to command them to keep the law of Moses;" and to circumcise as well as baptize. The circumcision, under these circumstances, was enjoined and received under the notion of being justified by the law; and became in its practical effect a sign of justification by the law. Under these circumstances, the apostles, divinely instructed, did with circumcision what Hezekiah did with "the brazen serpent that Moses had made," 2 Kings xviii. 14. It must no longer be tolerated when it became the means of sin and ruin. Paul also (Gal. v.) spoke against circumcision on the ground that they who practiced it, did it under the notion of attaining justification by the works of the law. To keep the seventh day, under the notion of being justified by the law, would put one equally off from the ground of grace. He would be "fallen from grace;" and "Christ should profit him nothing." It was on this ground that Paul interdicted circumcision, and on this only; for Paul himself (Acts xvi. 3), when he would have Timothy go forth with him, "took him and circumcised him, because of the Jews which were in those quarters."

So far, then, the covenant with its seal remain unimpaired by the giving and the removing of the law.

"Wherefore, then, serveth the law? It was added because of transgressions, till the seed should come, to whom the promise was made," Gal. iii. 19. The inference is inevitable; the law passes away when Christ comes, since it was only added to continue "till" that time. The promise and the covenant remain to be fulfilled; to wit, the promise referred to in these words, Gal. iii. 8, "And the Scripture, foreseeing that God would justify the heathen through faith, preached before the gospel unto Abraham, saying, In thee shall all the families of the earth be blessed."

If now WE were to add to this, "So, then, modern believers are built upon the foundation of the Abrahamic covenant," the reasoning might be questioned. But the word of God has come to such a conclusion, and it ought to seem to be no longer a matter to be questioned. "So, then," says the apostle, "they which be of faith, are blessed with faithful Abraham." "Know ye not, that they which are of faith, the same are the children of Abraham," Gal. iii. 7. Why are they not called the children of Enoch, or of Noah, or of Elijah, or of Moses? These men had faith, and were justified by faith. If simply to be justified by faith be the matter in which we are "Abraham's seed," can any mortal tell why we might not as well be called the seed of Enoch, or of Noah, or of Moses, or of Elijah? Plainly the COVENANT and its PROMISES are the reason why we are Abraham's seed: and Paul accordingly reasons on the ground of the covenant and the promise. But hear his conclusion, Gal. iii. 29, "And if ye be Christ's, then are ye Abraham's seed, and heirs according to the promise."

I might rest the argument here; but the word of God is not content to leave the matter so. It would make it so plain, "that he may run who readeth it." Thus, the prophets uniformly represent the kingdom of Zion, not as a *new* Church, but as Israel enlarged by the "bringing in" of the Gentiles. To say all that might be said in proof of this would be to repeat nearly all the passages in the prophets which speak of the kingdom of Christ. For your satisfaction I refer to chap. lx. of Isaiah, and onward through chap. lxv. Here is no casting away of God's people, and the erection of an entire new polity. It is Zion; it is Jerusalem that rises and shines; her light being come, and the glory of the Lord being risen upon her. The Gentiles come to her light, and kings to the brightness of her rising: "all they gather themselves and come to thee." These prophecies represent the Church of Jesus Christ in her course to universal empire over the earth: but it is still the ancient Zion and the ancient Jerusalem. It is still the covenant people of God, at a period when the promise is made sure to all the seed; "not to that only which is of the law, but that which is of faith;" to the Gentiles, upon whom the blessing of Abraham comes in the latter day.

The apostles are not less distinct in this matter than the prophets. Thus, Paul, Rom. xi. 25, "Blindness in part is happened unto Israel until the fulness of the Gentiles be come in." ("In?" Into what? To a house that is thrown down and cast away?) And more expressly in Eph. ii. 12–22, "Wherefore remember that ye, being in times past Gentiles in the flesh,"—"that at that time ye were without Christ, being aliens from the Commonwealth of Israel, and strangers from the covenant of promise, are made nigh by the blood of Christ. For he is our peace, who hath made both one, having broken down the middle wall of partition." "Now therefore ye are no more strangers and foreigners, but fellow citizens with the saints, and of the household of God; and are built upon the foundation of the apostles and prophets, Jesus Christ himself being the chief corner-stone."

I know there are those to whose scheme it is destruction, to consider the Abrahamic covenant as pertaining at all to us, or the Abrahamic and the Christian Church one and the same; and hence, when we mention these things, they profess that it is all unintelligible, and throw them by contemptuously as an idle and pernicious figment. But it seems to me, that we cannot throw these things away without throwing away the word of God. But as if the Scriptures had anticipated what objections would be raised, they go on, as though determined to put the matter beyond a question, if the clearest representations of holy writ can put any thing beyond question.

Thus, in Rom. xi., "God hath not cast away his people" whom he foreknew,—"there is a remnant,"—"the rest are blinded." "And if some of the branches be broken off" (mark! is the trunk destroyed when some of the branches are broken off?) "and thou, being a wild olive tree, wert graffed in among them" (graffed into nothing? and among nothing?) "and with them partakest of the root and fatness of the olive tree?" (Tell me, ye who are familiar with the process of engrafting, is the trunk torn up and cast away, when the scion is graffed in among its green branches, and with them partakes of its root and fatness?) "Boast not against the branches; but if thou boast, thou bearest not the root, but the root thee."

Can anything more strikingly and certainly assert

that the old trunk, the Abrahamic Church, is not thrown aside, but that the Christian Church draws its support and sustenance from the original and still living root, *the covenant of promise*, which secures us Christ; which secures us all the mercy that God has covenanted, or which comes to us through his Son? Could a voice from heaven, louder than seven thunders, and distinct as that which shall call the world to judgment, make this matter more plain?

One more passage of holy writ, and I have done on this point. The passage is in Rom. iv. 16, 17. "Therefore it is of faith, that it might be by grace; to the end the promise might be sure to all the seed; not to that only which is of the law, but to that also which is of the faith of Abraham, who is the father of us all; as it is written, I have made thee a father of many nations."

Here I rest under the first point, believing the proof to be plain and incontrovertible—resting on the sure authority of the word of God; that the Abrahamic and the Christian Church are one and the same; built upon the same covenant; saved with the same faith; considered in the word of God as one and the same Church.

I proceed to the second point.

II. *Circumcision and baptism are alike the seal of the same covenant, and the sign of the same thing.*

God appointed circumcision the seal of his covenant with Abraham in these words, Gen. xvii. 10: "This is my covenant, which ye shall keep between me and you, and thy seed after thee; Every man child shall be circumcised." Here circumcision is called the "covenant," by the common figure of placing the *sign* for the *thing*. Every one understands that literally circumcision is not the covenant, but the *token*, or *sign*, or *seal* of the covenant. That it is such a "sign" and "seal"—and what it signifies we are not left to conjecture.

Paul says, Rom. iv. 11, "He" (Abraham) "received the sign of circumcision, a seal of the righteousness of the faith which he had, yet being uncircumcised." A "sign!" a "seal!" of the righteousness of faith! Is not this "righteousness of faith" the very thing which Paul urges as the ground by which the sinner is justified, and has peace with God through our Lord Jesus Christ; of which "justification" he cites Abraham as an illustrious example? Of this "faith" Abraham received circumcision as the "seal." And what was the import of the seal? The renewal of the heart and of the spirit. This was the true circumcision, of which the outward circumcision was given as the sign, Rom. ii. 29: "Circumcision is that of the heart, in the spirit, and not in the letter." That is, the real thing denoted by the sign, circumcision—the truly being what circumcision should be the sign of being—is to be *cleansed in heart*. Of this it is the SIGN. Of the remission of sin and of the acceptance of the soul through the righteousness of faith it is the "SEAL."

Now baptism is the seal and sign of the same

things. Thus, Acts xxii. 16, "Arise and be baptized, and *wash away thy sins.*" The baptism does not literally "wash away sins;" but it is the sign, or token, or seal, of the washing away of sins; and of acceptance with God, in justification through the righteousness of faith. The real washing away of sins is accomplished with a bloody baptism—by the "sprinkling of the blood of Christ:" of this, baptism is the *seal*, in precisely the same manner as circumcision was the seal of the righteousness of faith; and the "sprinkling of blood is shadowed forth by the sprinkling of water."

And what is the import of this seal? What but the washing of the heart, and the inward cleansing by the Holy Spirit, which is called the "baptism of the Spirit?" As the circumcision of the heart was the work of the Holy Spirit, so here the baptism (or cleansing) of the heart, which is the work of the Holy Spirit, is called *"the washing of regeneration, and the renewing of the Holy Ghost,"* and this is shadowed forth by the "washing of water," or baptism: as it is said in Tit. iii. 5, "Christ loved the church, and gave himself for it, that he might sanctify and cleanse it with the washing of water by the word."

We have, then, *baptism* and *circumcision;* each a "*sign,*" each a "*seal,*" and each as a sign and as a seal signifying precisely the same thing.

But the word of God goes further, and expressly calls baptism the circumcision of Christ (or what is its precise equivalent, Christian circumcision). Thus, Col. ii. 11, 12, " In whom ye are circumcised, with the circumcision made without hands." Here is the real circumcision, the inward " circumcision of the heart and of the Spirit:" " the washing of regeneration, the renewing of the Holy Ghost"—" in putting off the body of the sins of the flesh, by the *circumcision of Christ:* buried with him *in baptism.*" Here is the outward circumcision of Christ (the sign of the inward)—baptism. Again, Phil. iii. 3, Christians are called "the circumcision," in allusion to their having wrought in them the thing signified by circumcision, and of which baptism under the dispensation of Christ is the outward sign. " For we are the circumcision, which worship God in the spirit, and rejoice in Christ Jesus, and have no confidence in the flesh."

The Abrahamic Church had a "seal" of the righteousness of faith. "The Christian Church is the same; has the Christian Church a seal of the righteousness of faith? If the Scriptures may be trusted, it has: baptism signifying the same thing as circumcision, and, in so many words, called the circumcision of Christ."

It is manifest, therefore, that baptism is substituted for circumcision:

IT IS A SEAL OF THE SAME COVENANT;
ORDAINED FOR THE SAME CHURCH;
IT MEANS THE SAME THING;
IT IS EMPLOYED FOR THE SAME USE;

WHILE CIRCUMCISION IS PASSED AWAY.

Here is the *reality of substitution*. If any dislike the word substitution, I care not to dispute for the word. Baptism is a sign, and but a sign; used as a seal; holding the same place; having the same meaning; fulfilling the same use; under the same covenant; and in the same Church: while circumcision is passed away. Here, then, is the reality of substitution. If any dislike the word, let the word be dropped: the reality remains, based upon the word of God. Baptism is now, what circumcision was once—a seal of the righteousness of faith, and of God's promise to be the God of such, and of their seed after them. Christianity has no other sign or seal of the righteousness of faith.*

Now what would those, who received the command to apply this new seal, understand with regard to the subjects to whom it was to be applied? They well understood the Abrahamic and the Christian Church to be one and the same: built on the same covenant, saved with the same faith, and re-

---

* It has been objected that circumcision was applied only to males. Might not this be among the reasons for a change of the seal? A distinction was made between male and female under the Mosaic dispensation, as between Jew and Greek, bond and free; but under Christ this distinction was abolished: "There is neither Jew nor Greek; there is neither bond nor free; there is neither male nor female." Hence—the seal remaining—there was a necessity for changing its form.

garded in the word of God as one and the same Church. Circumcision, the seal of the righteousness of faith, was by divine command, applied to children. When a Gentile was proselyted, the same seal was applied to him and to his children. In every covenant and promise of God, their children had been included: and this fact must have deeply impressed their minds, that everywhere throughout the law and the prophets, God was still accustomed to join in the same polity the parents and the children. To *exclude the children* is a strange thing, especially from a seal of the same covenant, which still retained in its promises the blessings promised to children. Here is a new seal of the same covenant—the same covenant, only enlarged, extending the blessing of Abraham to the Gentiles through faith.

Does the ratification and the enlargement of the covenant cut off the children, while nothing is revoked and nothing changed save the *form* of the seal? Here is a new form of the seal, but it has the same signification. The command is—"Go teach" (make disciples of) "all nations, baptizing them." Had the command been—go preach to the Gentiles—the "Gospel" which was before preached to Abraham, Gal. iii. 8—circumcising them; "he that believeth" and is circumcised "shall be saved," there could be no possibility of doubting that the infants of believing parents are to be included. But how is the case altered when they are to apply another sign of the same design and signification? Is the case altered at all? Will they not understand it as referring to the same subjects? So they must naturally understand it: such would be its inevitable interpretation, unless there were an express exception of such infants in the command. Without some warrant, it is, methinks, impossible that the disciples would presume to take away from parents and children the privileges granted to them by the charter of Jehovah. These of necessity stand till Jehovah himself takes them away. The chartered privileges remaining to them, the seal of that charter, as it was once theirs, would remain, even though the form of the seal be changed.

This has been illustrated by a homely similitude, and yet a similitude so much in point that I will copy it.

A man orders his servants to mark the sheep of his flock with a bloody sign, and is careful to add, see that you apply this sign to all the lambs also. Afterwards, he sees fit to dispense with the bloody sign made with a knife in the flesh, and ordains that his servants mark his sheep with paint; but he says nothing about the lambs. Will those servants, because the marking is a "positive institution," argue that the lambs are no longer to be marked? As they buy more sheep with lambs, will they mark the sheep, but say they have no warrant for marking the lambs? The contrary. And so, from the very circumstances of the case, the disciples of Christ, understanding the design and import of baptism, and having been previously accustomed to extend another sign, of the same import and use, to children, would naturally interpret the command to baptize, as implying the baptism of infants.

Had it been objected, that men are to *believe* and be baptized; and that even "saving faith" is to go before baptism in the case of adults, they would still remember that infants could no more believe in Abraham's day than they can now; and yet, at God's command, they received "circumcision, a seal of the righteousness of faith;" and that the objection would have had precisely the same force against circumcision then, that it has against baptism now. They would have remembered, moreover, that if the want of a capacity for "believing" should hinder baptism, the same reason would prove that they cannot be saved: since the Gospel says, "He that believeth and is baptized, shall be saved;" "He that be'ieveth not shall be damned;" and infants cannot believe. But a reasoning which proves too much, and proves what is false, proves nothing at all, and the objection falls to the ground.

Another circumstance would have had weight upon their minds in all questions touching the relations of children under the Gospel dispensation. Some parents once brought little children (infants, says Luke xviii. 15) to Christ, that he should lay his hands on them and bless them. His disciples forbade them. They understood that Christ's kingdom was to rest upon faith in the soul, and upon the intelligent obedience of men to his precepts; but how could children have this faith or this knowledge? They appear to have come to the same conclusion concerning bringing little children to Christ that he might *touch* them, that many in these days arrive at concerning the baptism of little children;—"what good can it do to an unconscious babe?" At all events, they forbade these parents to bring their infants to Christ for this purpose. But Christ rebuked them; he called the little children to him; he took them in his arms; he blessed them; he said, "Suffer little children to come unto me, and forbid them not: for of such is the kingdom of Heaven." He meant by the kingdom of Heaven, either his earthly Church or his heavenly; it matters not which for the argument. If the heavenly Church is, in part, made up of such, then this was a sufficient reason for Christ why he should take them in his arms and bless them, and rebuke those who would forbid them to be brought to him. It is the very reason that he alleged, and he himself drew these conclusions from the reason. What an argument for bringing little children to Christ now—that he may seal them as his own; and that visibly as he did when he took them in his arms! But if by "Kingdom of Heaven" he meant his "earthly Church," then the argument is at an end: they are to be baptized on this express warrant.

Those who wish to prevent this passage from

bearing on the question at issue say, that by the words " of such," our Lord meant—not of such infants, but of such " simple-hearted and humble persons" is the kingdom of heaven. This would be a good reason why " simple-hearted and humble persons" should not be forbidden to come to Christ; but the fact that " simple-hearted and humble" adults belong to the kingdom of God, is no reason why Christ should take *infants* in his arms and bless *them*.

It is said, we forget that Jesus did not *baptize* them. No, we do not forget that " Jesus himself baptized not—but his disciples." It is not necessary for us to assert or to suppose that these infants were baptized at all. Christ's disciples were sent at first to preach, not a Redemption completed, but to preach, saying, " The kingdom of heaven is at *hand*." Their final commission was after the resurrection of our Lord ; and at that time he instituted his baptism, which appears to be essentially different from that practiced before. The disciples of Christ baptized newly made disciples before this, but it seems to have been John's " baptism of repentance," Acts xix. 4, and not the baptism instituted by Christ as the new seal of his covenant.

Grant it, if our brethren please, that these infants were not baptized.* This conduct of Christ, and

---

* Though as much is said of their baptism as there is of the baptism of any particular adults from this time forward

this rebuke which he administered to those who would forbid infants, would at least teach his disciples no more to reject infants from the blessings of the Christian religion, under the notion that infants cannot believe. It would teach them no more to forbid parents to bring them to Christ for his blessing. It would teach them to be cautious how they forbade infants from the privileges which God had chartered to them in his covenant. It was designed to teach them how Christ regarded infants; and the remembrance of this would necessarily bear upon the interpretation which they would give with regard to the application of the new seal, whether to apply it to infants or not.

But how they did in fact interpret the law, I come now to show under the third head.

III. *That the children of believers, as they were connected with the Abrahamic Church, are recognized in the New Testament as sustaining the same relation to the Christian Church.*

"For the unbelieving husband is sanctified by the wife, and the unbelieving wife is sanctified by the husband, else were your children unclean, but now are they holy." 1 Cor. vii. 14. Of course this cannot mean that the children are spiritually holy, simply because one of the parents is a believer.

---

during the life of Christ, or indeed during the previous part of his ministry, no particular cases are mentioned. Silence in one case proves as much as in another.

The word "holy" here is the opposite of "unclean," with which it is contrasted. And the word unclean (the same in the original language as well as ours) is used in Acts x. 14, 15, 28, and Acts xi. 3, 8, 9, in a way which fully explains the use of it here. Peter was to be prepared to go and instruct and baptize Cornelius, a Gentile. A vision was given him, of a great sheet, knit at the four corners, wherein were all manner of four-footed beasts, and creeping things, and fowls of the air. And there came a voice to him, saying, "Rise, Peter, kill and eat." But Peter said, "Not so, Lord, for I have never eaten anything that is common or *unclean*." And the voice spoke to him again: "What God hath cleansed that call not thou common." So Peter answered the messenger of Cornelius, "God hath showed me that I should not call any man *common* or *unclean*." But for going to Cornelius, a Gentile, they that were of the circumcision contended with him (as Peter might have done with another man, had he not been better instructed by the vision)—saying, "thou wentest in to men uncircumcised, and didst eat with them." Then Peter rehearsed the matter from the beginning, and told how the voice answered from heaven, saying, "What God hath cleansed, that call not thou common." The point is this: to the Israelites the Gentiles had been considered as unclean, out of the pale of their society, and debarred from the covenant and worship of the people of God: or, as Paul expresses

16

it, Eph. ii. 12-22, "Gentiles in the flesh — strangers from the covenant of promise."

With this explanation turn to the passage under consideration—"else were your children *unclean*"— cut off from the commonwealth of Christ's visible Church, and debarred from the seal of the covenant, as Pagans; or, as says Matthew Henry, "They would be heathen, out of the pale of the Church and covenant of God." The Apostle bases his argument upon a fact which he assumes as well known and universally recognized in practice; that the children of believing parents are so far a "Holy seed," — and in that sense "holy" (as opposed to "unclean"),—that they are entitled to the covenant privileges belonging to the "household" of faith. Doddridge says (and with him agree the great mass of the most distinguished commentators, as well as the great mass of the Christian world)—"On the maturest and the most impartial consideration of this text, I must refer it to Infant Baptism."

Indeed, this is the natural interpretation of the passage, and the most rigid scrutiny of the use of the words in the original language not only bears out this interpretation, but condemns every other that has been advanced. And so surely does this natural interpretation prove Infant Baptism to be an ordinance of God, that opposers of the ordinance have felt that there is no relief but to set aside the interpretation. I have read many subtle and earnest comments and essays, written with much talent and pains, to set aside this interpretation; but I have not yet found one which attempts to reconcile it with a denial of the ordinance.

The many ingenious, jarring and mutually destructive glosses, which have been put upon this passage to avoid the dreaded conclusion, show how sensibly they feel the difficulty; and how hard they find it to hit upon one which shall seem tenable or plausible to all even among themselves. The one most commonly received and relied on is that of the famous Dr. Gill; which supposes the Apostle to mean, "Else were your children *illegitimate*, but now are they *legitimate*." The absurdities of this gloss are manifold and palpable. It is sufficient to mention one or two. 1. The terms which he renders "legitimate" and "illegitimate" have no such meaning anywhere else in any author, sacred or profane; of course the rendering is a sheer invention—the effort of a subtle wit to extricate itself from an unpleasant difficulty. It is impossible that those to whom the Apostle wrote should understand him to mean so. It would be just as much to the point, and no grosser license, to render the word, "Else were your children *cripples*, but now are they *sound*." 2. The gloss proceeds upon the ineffable absurdity of proving the lawfulness of the marriage by the legitimacy of the children. A conclusion, to avoid which such absurdities must be encountered, is surely irresistible.

While the substance of this gloss is retained in

the text of the "*Scripture Guide to Baptism,*" published by the "Baptist General Tract Society," another gloss is introduced in a note (in some editions, in the Appendix) by the authority of the "Directors" of the Society. Both glosses cannot, of course, be true. By which they intend to abide, I know not—whether by the text or note; or which they wish us to receive and hold as the truth; or whether to plant a foot on each, as doubting whether either is sound: or whether to retain both, that one may meet some minds that are not met by the other. The *note* proposes to consider the passage not as referring to the lawfulness of the marriage or to the legitimacy or the illegitimacy of the children, but to consider it as though the argument were, *If a believer put away a wife or a husband as an unbeliever, he must put away his children also.* But this is not the argument. The argument of the Apostle is the reverse of this. He *assumes* that the children are holy or clean; and from this fact assumed as admitted and well known, he convinces the Corinthians that the believing husband need not put away his unbelieving wife, since, in that case, a consequence would follow, which (he assumes) THEY KNOW CANNOT FOLLOW. The argument of the ritual holiness of the children, is based upon the fact of such children's having been treated as a "Holy seed" connected with the Church of God. The reference, in such case, can be no other than to Infant Baptism so notoriously practiced in the Church.

I cannot but think, had the Apostle meant to say what the note represents him as saying, that rather than leaving that meaning to be inferred by a course of reasoning which requires so many ages to produce one mind even to guess it out, he would have said so directly, instead of using the circuitous way of talking about "unclean" and "holy;" words which would naturally mislead his hearers, which actually misled the ancient church, as well as so many modern believers, and indeed the great mass of the whole Christian world; for in truth there are as yet few even among the Baptists, that have ever understood the passage according to the tenor of the note in question.

The common interpretation, therefore, stands: and I adduce this text as evidence that as the children of believers had been joined in covenant privileges with the Abrahamic Church, they are recognized in the New Testament as sustaining the same relation to the Christian Church.

Turn now to another source of argument. But first let me make some preliminary remarks to show the value of the evidence, and to vindicate it from objections that have been raised against it.

The *Sabbath* was instituted at the creation: and though *weeks* are mentioned in the sacred history, the Sabbath is not again mentioned till Moses: yet how important the Sabbath was considered in the sight of God is well known. Again, it is not mentioned from the time of Joshua till the reign of David, and yet (as says Dr. Humphrey), "It will be admitted that, beyond all doubt, the pious Judges of Israel remembered the Sabbath day to keep it holy." Moreover, the Bible says nothing of *circumcision* from a little after Moses till the days of Jeremiah, a period of eight hundred years; yet doubtless circumcision was practised all the while.

In like manner, our Missionary Herald, each volume of which is twenty times as large as the book of Acts, is now in the progress of the thirty-sixth volume.* In the whole of these, containing the journals of so many Missionaries, narrating every important incident with so much minuteness, and continued for so many years, there are very few instances mentioned of Infant Baptism. I have not the means at hand of ascertaining how many, but though I have been long familiar with them, and have long observed the fact with some curiosity, and have specially examined not a little, I am not able to find or call to mind more than a very few instances previously to the last two years. But we know that the Missionaries of the American Board are all Pedobaptists. The paucity of these records of infant baptism in their letters does not prove that they do not baptize infants : we know they do; and once in a while the fact is mentioned, but it is rare, though their converts amount to many thousands.

Suppose now, that, at the present time, you find

---

* A. D. 1840.

a pamphlet of twenty or thirty pages, like a single monthly number of the Missionary Herald, only half as large — covering the ground of some fifty years, and giving an account of the doings of certain Missionaries of whom you have never heard before. The question is asked, Are they Baptist Missionaries: or do they baptize the infant children of believing parents? On examining the pamphlet, we find such records as these: at such a time "I baptized—in the night—a Jailor and all his;" at such a time "Lydia and her household;" at such a time "I baptized also the household of Stephanus." Nothing is said as to whether they were all adults, or whether, as is more common, there were children in these households. Only this is certain, that if there were children, they were certainly baptized. Suppose further, that at this crisis we discover copious letters of these Missionaries, written to their converts from heathenism, in which letters they use the term household just as we do the word family. Are they Baptist Missionaries? The presumption is that they are not. You find a difficulty which must be removed before you can believe that they are Baptists. Moreover, you take the journals of the Baptist Missionaries of fifty or a hundred times the size of this newly discovered pamphlet, and a hundred times more full. You do not learn that they ever give an account of the baptism of a single *household;* though you can understand how desirable it would be to make such a record as frequent in their journals as possible: and how readily they would be brought forward in argument as often as they might occur.

You now make another discovery, viz.: that these unknown Missionaries consider the Abrahamic and the Christian Church the same. Now let one passage be found in a single letter of theirs to one of their Churches gathered from heathenism, to this effect: "The unbelieving wife is sanctified by the husband, and the unbelieving husband is sanctified by the wife, else were your children *unclean*, but now are they *holy;*" let it be proved that they familiarly use these terms in the Jewish sense; let but one such passage as this be found, and the question is settled — THEY BAPTIZE CHILDREN.

Who could ask for more convincing proof, unless he is determined that nothing shall prove it, save an express declaration in so many words, or a miracle? I might appeal to any man accustomed to sifting and weighing evidence in our courts of justice, is not this valid proof of the fact? Were it a question of fact to be decided by mere impartial jurors in our courts of law, whether these Missionaries practised Infant Baptism, could there be a doubt how, on this evidence, the question would be decided? Could there be a doubt that the verdict would be, *These men believe in Infant Baptism and practise it?*

Make it known now that these men are the Apostles of our Lord, acting under the guidance of the

Holy Spirit; and the interpretation of the law of baptism, which extends baptism to the infants of believing parents, has a *divine warrant;* and *Infant Baptism is an ordinance of God.*

Strong as this evidence is, it is further corroborated in the fact,

IV. *That the whole Church received infant baptism—as several of the early fathers declare, and as the Church at large believed—from the Apostles; and that the whole Church, together with all sects of heretics, practised it, with not a man to raise his voice against its divine warrant for more than thirty generations after Christ.*

Some of the Apostles and evangelists were spared to the Church a long time, and the interval between the last of them and the earliest of the Christian fathers is very brief. Thus, Peter and Paul lived till about A. D. 68; Jude, Thomas, and Luke till about A. D. 74; and John lived till about A. D. 100.

Before this last date Justin Martyr was born, in the midst of Christians, at Neapolis, in Samaria. About forty years after the death of John, he published his first Apology for the Christians, addressed to Antoninus Pius. In that Apology he says, "Many persons of both sexes, some sixty, some seventy years old, were made disciples to Christ *from childhood*" (ἐκ παιδων). On this passage President Dwight justly remarks that "there never was any other mode of making disciples from infancy except by baptism." Dr. Pond also says, "they were doubtless made such (disciples) by baptism;" for the same word, "made disciples," (εμαθετευθησαν), is used by Christ in the commission, "Go and disciple all nations, baptizing them."

Irenæus was born about the time of Justin. He was a pupil of Polycarp of Smyrna, who had been a pupil of the Apostle John. Irenæus says, "I can describe the spot on which Polycarp sat and expounded; his going in and coming out; the manner of his life; the figure of his body; the sermons he preached to the multitudes; how he related to us his converse with John, and the rest of those who had seen the Lord; how he mentioned their particular expressions, and what things he had heard from them of the Lord; of his miracles and of his doctrines." Irenæus says, "Christ came to save all persons by himself; all I say, who by him are regenerated unto God; *infants*, and little ones, and youths, and elder persons." He constantly employs the term regenerated for baptized, and so means here: thus, when speaking of our Lord's authorizing his Apostles to baptize, he says,* "When he gave his disciples the power of regenerating unto God, he said unto them, Go teach all nations, baptizing them." Justin uses the term in the same sense; speaking of the baptism of the Christian converts, he says, "They are conducted by us to a place where there is water,

---

* Gray, p. 58.

and are regenerated in the same manner in which we were regenerated; for they are then washed in the name of God the Father and Lord of the universe, and of our Saviour Jesus Christ, and of the Holy Spirit."

Whether these fathers meant by "regenerated," what some later ones did mean, that baptism confers an inward regeneration, so that those who are baptized are simultaneously and inwardly regenerated by the Holy Ghost, it is foreign to my purpose now to inquire. Whatever were their views of doctrine, they are certainly good witnesses with regard to a matter of *fact*, viz., whether infants were in their day baptized; and such is the clear import of their testimony.

Tertullian was born a little later than Irenæus, about A. D. 145. He ran into all manner of vagaries of doctrine; but this invalidates not his testimony with regard to a matter of fact, whether the Church in his day baptized infants. He advises the delay of baptism not only in the case of children, but of youths and unmarried people. In the case of little children he says, "For what need, except in case of necessity, that their godfathers should be in danger?" Because they may "either fail of their promises by death, or they may be deceived by a child's proving of a wicked disposition." He supposed that the act of baptism washed away sins; and therefore would have not only infants, but youth and unmarried persons delay, till they should be less exposed to temptations, that they might have the greater benefit of the baptism, and have a smaller score of sins to answer for afterwards. He says of infants: "What need their innocent age make such haste to the forgiveness of sins" (viz., by baptism). He thus fully recognizes the practice of Infant Baptism as in common use. "*And speaks against it,*" say our Baptist brethren. True, he does; but he speaks against it as against a thing in common use. The question is not whether Tertullian is against it or for it; but whether it was in use in his day. He does not pretend that baptism is an innovation, or unlawful, or that it had not been in use from the days of the Apostles. He pleads for delay, on the ground of advantage, and on the same ground pleads that youths and unmarried persons would be gainers by delay. He places the reason for delay, in both instances, on the same ground. But surely our Baptist brethren will not receive his reasons for delay in either case. His testimony to the fact remains; the more unquestionable for its being incidental, and for his whimsical bias against it.

Origen was born 185 years after Christ. In his homily on Luke xiv. he says, "*Infants are baptized for the forgiveness of sins.*" Again, in his homily on Levit. viii., he says, "What is the reason why the baptism of the Church, which is given for the remission for sins, is by the usage of the Church given to infants also?" He is endeavoring to establish the doctrine of original sin, and adduces the practice of Infant Baptism as a proof of it. Again, in his comment on Romans: "For this also it was, that the Church had from the Apostles a tradition to give baptism to infants."

Ambrose, Chrysostom, Cyprian, and Gregory Nazianzen speak expressly of the practice of Infant Baptism.

Augustine, in reference to the Pelagians, says, "Since they grant that infants must be baptized, as not being able to resist the authority of the Church *which was doubtless delivered by our Lord and his Apostles*, they must consequently grant that they stand in need of the benefit of the mediator."

Again, Augustine against the Donatists, speaking of the baptism of infants, says, "Which the whole body of the Church holds, *as delivered to them*, in the case of little infants baptized; and yet no Christian man will say they are baptized to no purpose."*

Augustine again: "The custom of our mother Church in baptizing infants must not be disregarded nor accounted needless, nor believed to be anything else than an ordinance delivered to us *from the Apostles*."†

Again, he declares that he "never met with any Christian, either of the general Church or of any of the sects, nor with any writer who owned the authority of the Scriptures, who taught any other doctrine than that infants are to be baptized for the

---

* Miller on Baptism, p. 37.   † Dr. Miller, pp. 36, 37.

remission of sin." He declares that it was not instituted by councils, but was always in use.*

Now, in opposition to the testimony of these witnesses, we have the tract: "THE SCRIPTURE GUIDE TO BAPTISM," published by "The General Baptist Tract Society," and this tract says, "*Our* principles are as old as Christianity. Persons holding our distinctive principles, *i. e.* the baptism of believers only, have appeared in all ages of the Christian era. From Christ to nearly the end of the second century, there were NO OTHERS" (the word "no others" in capitals); "at least, if there were any, their history is a blank. After Infant Baptism was introduced, many opposed it." So says this tract by Pengilly.

Round assertion! But on what proof? Not a scrap is offered; and that for the best of all reasons, there is no such evidence in the world. It has been sought; most ardently has it been longed for; but there is none; no—none even to hang a pretence upon. It is *asserted* that none practiced Infant Baptism till near the end of the second century; but do they pretend to tell how it was introduced then, and that so quietly as to be everywhere received in Europe and Asia, and all along the coast of Africa, and throughout the Christian world; and nobody know but that they had always practiced it from the days of the Apostles! No—not one poor lisp; not a syllable to show how or when it was introduced!

---

* Dr. Miller, pp. 36, 37.

INFANT BAPTISM. 195

It is asserted, that " when it was introduced, many did not receive it, and many opposed it." Who did not receive it? The Fathers declare they never heard of such a man; nor do our Baptist brethren attempt to say who. Who opposed it? Echo answers, Who? Our Baptist brethren do not attempt to tell. But the "General Tract Society" of the denomination send out this Tract to assert in round terms that "to nearly the end of the second century, there were no others" than Baptists on the question of baptizing infants, and, that " after Infant Baptism was introduced, many opposed it !"*

---

* Our Baptist brethren also claim that the Waldenses, those venerable witnesses for the truth, maintain their views and rejected infant baptism. If this were so, it would not at all affect the argument, nor refute the matter already in proof, viz., that for four hundred years after Christ infant baptism was everywhere practiced in the Christian church. But the Waldenses did not reject infant baptism. Their own confession of faith, drawn up between the twelfth century and the period of the Reformation, expressly declares that they present their children—infants—for baptism; and they declare that their faith and usages had been handed down from father to son for several hundred years. Dr. Murdock, in his notes on Mosheim, vol. iii. p. 228, 229, declares that at the time of the rejection of infant baptism by the Mennonites and the Anti-Pedobaptist sects of that age, the Waldenses of France and Bohemia were "universally believers in infant baptism." When their Popish neighbors charged them with denying the baptism of infants, they repelled the charge, and said, "Yet notwithstanding, we bring our children to be baptized."

But let us go on with the testimony. Pelagius denied the doctrine of original sin, and was pressed with the absurdity of Infant Baptism on his principles. Could he have denied Infant Baptism, or shown it to be a corruption, it would have relieved him from his difficulties and given him a signal triumph. He was a man of great abilities and great learning, and had travelled the Christian world over. He and his coadjutor, Celestius, used every means to relieve themselves from the pressure of the question, "Why are infants baptized for the remission of sins, if they have none?" With this argument, says Dr. Pond, "Pelagius and his abettors were much embarrassed, and had recourse to a variety of evasions in order to escape from it." But they never denied infant baptism. They never pretended that it was a corruption or innovation. On the contrary, Pelagius says, "Baptism ought to be administered to infants with the same sacramental words which are used in the case of adults." "Men slander me," said he, "as if I denied the sacrament of baptism to infants;" and again, "I NEVER HEARD OF ANY, *not even the most impious heretic*, WHO DENIED BAPTISM TO INFANTS."*

It is easy to see, from these extracts, that the Christian Church early slid away from purity in doctrine, and that many of the old Fathers were not very sound theologians. I adduce them not to prove

---

* Dr. Pond on Baptism, p. 107.

a point in theology by their opinion; I adduce them, not to build Infant Baptism on their authority; I adduce them as witnesses to a matter of fact:—that from the time of the Apostles, Infant Baptism was everywhere practiced and understood to have been received from the Apostles, with no man anywhere to lisp a breath in favor of a contrary supposition; but with the unbroken and uniform belief that its authority rested on a foundation none other than the practice of apostles who were inspired of God.

If it had ever been a corrupt innovation, would there not have been somewhere some controversy about it? Would all, everywhere, have so unanimously agreed to receive it? Would every trace of such innovation or such controversy have perished from history; so that men living near the Apostolic age, though under the strongest inducement to seek out such history, had it existed, could never be able to find the least trace or fragment of it, or even to suspect its existence! Could these things be so? Can you believe them to be so? Can you stretch your credulity to that point with ever so great an effort? But unless what is so improbable and incredible be certainly true, then Infant Baptism was practiced by the Apostles, and rests for its authority upon the authority of God. Now we know how to interpret the command, "Go and teach (disciple) all nations, *baptizing* them;"—it means, "Baptize believers and their infant children." It means, to observe the order of the ancient

17*

covenant: which made God the God of believers and of their seed after them. A flood of light is thrown upon the interpretation of such passages as represent Christ as taking little children in his arms, and saying, "Of such is the kingdom of heaven." It corroborates our understanding of those narratives which speak of the baptism of households. It corroborates the natural interpretation of that passage which says, "The unbelieving husband is sanctified by the wife, and the unbelieving wife is sanctified by the husband, else were your children unclean, but now are they holy." One by one we have taken up these stones fitted by the chisel. They match together. We build on. They grow into an arch, as if formed by the Great Master Builder with that design. Not a stone is wanting. The keystone is driven. Each stone lends its aid to strengthen the whole. The work is complete. It stands; it will stand eternally; and round its circling brow is graven as in letters sunk deep in the enduring rock, and illumined by the rays of heaven:—"THE BAPTISM OF THE INFANT CHILDREN OF BELIEVING PARENTS, RESTS FOR ITS FOUNDATION UPON NO LESS A BASIS THAN THE AUTHORITY OF GOD."

V.

INFANT BAPTISM.

OBJECTIONS ANSWERED: ITS UTILITY VINDICATED.

What advantage, then, hath the Jew? or what profit is there of circumcision? Much every way: chiefly because that unto them were committed the oracles of God. For what if some did not believe? shall their unbelief make the faith of God without effect?—ROMANS iii. 1-3.

THE authority of Infant Baptism we have already considered. I shall now proceed to ANSWER SOME OBJECTIONS WHICH HAVE BEEN URGED AGAINST THE PRACTICE, AND TO VINDICATE ITS UTILITY.

It is asked, "*What good can it do to sprinkle an unconscious babe?*"

If this be asked with regard to the effect of the bare act of sprinkling, I answer, no good. Nor does the bare act of baptizing an adult do any good, through any virtue in the act, sprinkle—pour—plunge—wash—scour—do what you will. The bare *act* has no virtue in it; and the bare water does no good, whatever be the mode of applying it; and no matter whether the subject of it be conscious or unconscious.

But if God has commanded it, as a token—as a seal of his covenant—as a means of keeping parents and children and the world in mind of the great truth that the *sins* need to be washed away by "the sprinkling of the blood of Christ;" and that the polluted soul, even of the infant, needs the "washing of regeneration and the renewing of the Holy Ghost;" if God sees fit to appoint it as a sign of his covenant, as he appointed the bow in the cloud for the encouragement of men in another respect; if he sees fit to appoint it for its salutary influence upon the parent's heart, to encourage his prayers and his efforts for the spiritual good of his child; or if he sees fit to appoint it as an encouragement to piety by putting honor upon the piety of parents; or if to make his claim to the soul of that child, and, by affixing his seal, to challenge of him who has received it, love and duty through all the remainder of his life; or for whatever unknown and secret reason other than these, God has seen fit to appoint the sign :— then it does good to obey God, even if there is no good done by the bare act of baptizing an unconscious babe. Doubtless there are wise and important reasons. Some important uses we can see and feel; and though the baptism be not on the infant's faith, yet how often did the Saviour grant healing to diseased children, on account of the faith and importunity of the parents; as in the case of the Syrophenician woman, and of the Centurion, whose faith brought healing even to his afflicted servant?

The inquiry then, "What good can it do to the unconscious babe," in the first place, proceeds upon a ground which none of us, not even the objector, holds otherwise than as idle and false; viz., that the bare act of baptizing, of itself, does good to anybody. In the second place, it is an appeal not to piety, but to infidelity. In the third place, it proposes to men to inquire concerning what they hold as an ordinance of Jehovah, "What good can it do?" And if the question could carry its aim, and establish its principle, it would lead men to reject any command of God, the reasons of which are not plain to their understanding. On this ground Abraham would never have left his father's house; he would never have proceeded to offer up his son for a burnt offering.

Surely we shall not be driven from faith and duty by this illogical and infidel objection, how often soever our brethren may see fit to sound it in our ears! Surely it is not good to disobey God under the notion that he has required what can do no good! How easy would it have been to ask the same question with regard to *circumcising infants!* How easy to pour out a torrent of ribaldry upon "*such*" an ordinance as "doing good" to an unconscious babe! How many worse things might have been said of it than are said of the ordinance which we sometimes hear ridiculed under the name of "baby sprinkling!" Should the Patriarchs and their posterity therefore set it aside, and suffer themselves to be jeered out of God's covenant promises for their children?

But again it is asked, "*Do you believe that infants are lost if they die unbaptized?*" No, no, no! We believe no such thing; we fear no such thing. But shall we take it for granted that our infants are to die in infancy, and therefore disobey God, and exhibit our contempt for his covenant? If, peradventure, they should *live*, can we be sure that no effects of our disobedience and unbelief may come down upon them, either by the natural influence of that unbelief, or by the special displeasure of God upon those who break his covenant? Or, if we may be sure of this, is it certainly best to disobey God?

But again it is asked, "*Do you think baptism a regenerating and saving ordinance?* Do you think it sure that the children whom you baptize will ever be converted and saved; at least in consequence of the baptism? And if not, to what profit is the baptism, if it neither converts nor ensures future conversion; and if multitudes who are baptized are never converted or saved?"

If we could not answer particularly to these inquiries, it would still be enough to be able to give this answer: "*God has so instructed us;*" and it would be quite as good an answer as Abraham could have given when he was about to do a greater thing, and when much harder questions might have been asked concerning the propriety of the act; to wit, when Abraham was about to offer up his son Isaac as a burnt offering.

But Paul shall answer these inquiries in detail. Objectors argued of old as objectors argue now; and while they meant no such thing, they have caused the Bible to be made all the richer; just as all errors and heresies, and all the objections of infidels, subsequent to the age of revelation, have only served to bring out the truth more clear and glorious than it ever would have appeared in the eyes of the world. Who knows but these objections were made, and answered, and recorded, to meet just such emergencies as these? Who knows but that God designs, through the spirited and persevering efforts by which our Baptist brethren shake the minds of some, and overthrow the faith of others, to establish his truth and his ordinances the more firmly, and to let his Church see more clearly than otherwise they ever would have seen the Divine warrant, and the large benefits of his covenant, and of the application of its seal to their infant children?

The objection is, "*That the ordinance does neither convert, nor ensure conversion; that many who receive it are never converted in their lives; and that it seems useless, if not a mockery, to apply a seal significant of inward cleansing, and implying a covenant of spiritual blessings to those who have not, and may never have the reality.*"

I think I have stated the objections as fully and as strongly as any can desire.

Paul shall answer it, and turn the tables upon the objector, by more thoroughly establishing the point than if it had never been questioned.

In Rom. ii. he has been showing the Jew that neither the law, nor the covenant, nor its seal, nor its promises, can save him, without his own personal faith; and by that same faith the Gentile may be saved as well as the Jew. Nay more, all the seals and privileges are *null* to the Jew if he be a " breaker of the law ;" and if the Gentile keep the law, it shall be with him as though he had been circumcised. Thus, verses 25, 26 : " But if thou be a breaker of the law, thy circumcision is made uncircumcision; therefore, if the uncircumcision keep the righteousness of the law, shall not his uncircumcision be counted for circumcision ;" and verses 28, 29 : " For he is not a Jew (*i. e.* a child of God), which is one outwardly : neither is that circumcision which is outward in the flesh; but he is a Jew which is one inwardly ;-and circumcision is that of the heart, in the spirit and not in the letter, whose praise is not of men but of God."

Here the conditions are as are supposed in the objection against Infant Baptism. Those *with* the seal shall not be saved without their own personal qualifications; and those *without* the seal shall be saved with those qualifications. It is one God who shall justify the *circumcision* by faith, and the uncircumcision through faith. Moreover, the seal is applied to those who are not converted by it, and many of them are not converted at all. Moreover, the seal is one significant of inward cleansing, "in the heart and in the spirit," and so connected with a covenant which has salvation for its end.

The conditions are precisely the same as those supposed in the objections against Infant Baptism. Why apply a seal of such a signification, and of *such* a covenant, to them who are not inwardly cleansed by it, and who may never be converted at all? Is it not mockery? At least is it not useless?

Paul had either heard the objection made, or his natural forecast taught him it would be made; or rather, the Holy Ghost, to answer all such objections then and for ever, caused the objection to be started in the form of this inquiry, Rom. iii. 1–3: "*What advantage then hath the Jew? Or what profit is there of circumcision?*" (viz. if the circumcision does not convert him, nor ensure that he shall be converted; and if the circumcised person cannot be saved on other conditions than the uncircumcised?) "Much every way," answers the Apostle. Chiefly because that unto them were committed the oracles of God. *For what if some did not believe?* (It was with the circumcised as with the baptized, some did not believe; and the unbelievers were lost as much as though they had been uncircumcised; just as unbelievers will be lost, though they may have been baptized.) "For what if some did not believe? shall their unbelief make the faith of God of none effect? God forbid; yea, let God be true, but every man a liar."

The unbelief of some then is no objection against the covenant of God, or against his faithfulness to that covenant, and notwithstanding the objection, there is every way much profit of circumcision. It was still the seal of God's covenant. A score of centuries after Jehovah's promise to be the God of Abraham and his seed, the seed of Abraham, "as touching the election," were "beloved for the fathers' sake." "And because he loved thy fathers, he chose their seed after them;" and (Deut. vii.) "Know, therefore, that the Lord thy God he is God, the faithful God, which keepeth covenant and mercy with them that love him and keep his commandments, to a thousand generations."

The blessings of this covenant, it was foretold, should come upon the Gentiles. Abraham was to be the "father of *many nations.*" The promise was to be "sure to *all the seed,* not only to that which is of the law, but to that which is of faith." Nay, the prophets who foretold the glory of Christ's kingdom, when they spake in the most glowing strains, made mention of this same arrangement under the dispensation of Christ. Thus, Isa. lxv. 17, and onward: "For behold I create new heavens and a new earth: and the former shall not be remembered, nor come into mind. But be ye glad, and rejoice for ever in that which I create: for behold I create Jerusalem a rejoicing and her people a joy." "They shall not labor in vain, nor bring forth for trouble, for they are the seed of the blessed of the Lord, AND THEIR OFFSPRING WITH THEM."

Well might the Apostle Peter cry out, "For *the promise is to you*, AND TO YOUR CHILDREN, and to all that are afar off, even as many as the Lord our God shall call." Well might Paul declare, "And if ye are Christ's, then are ye Abraham's seed, and heirs according to the promise."

God appears to have designed to make a large use of the *family influence* in establishing and perpetuating the Gospel of salvation; in keeping alive on the earth Gospel truth and Gospel ordinances. For this reason he ordained that the marriage relation should be limited to one husband and one wife. Thus, Mal. ii. 14, 15, "Yet is she thy companion and the wife of thy covenant. And did He not make one? Yet had He the residue of the Spirit. And wherefore *one?* THAT HE MIGHT SEEK A GODLY SEED."

For the same end he established his covenant in the household of Abraham. "For I know him," said the Lord, "*that he will command his children and his household after him;* and they shall keep the way of the Lord, to do justice and judgment, that the Lord may bring upon Abraham that which he hath spoken of him."

On the same principle it is said, Ps. lxxviii. 5-7, "For He established a testimony in Jacob, and appointed a law in Israel, which he commanded our fathers that they should make them known to their children; that the generation to come might know them, even the children which should be born, who should arise and teach them to their children; that they might set their hope in God, and not forget the works of God, but keep his commandments."

God was pleased to ordain that his blessing and the fruits of pious labor and of prayer should go together; *and he graciously established and sealed this ordinance by covenant.* The reason for the covenant and the seal remaining, they remain. They remain enlarged and ratified in Christ to the end of time. Shall we be told that it does no good to remember this covenant? no good, as we look on the seal, to let the promise of the covenant encourage our hearts, and quicken our prayers? Has the Lord mistaken his appointment, and given an unnecessary covenant and a useless seal? Shall we conclude so? Shall we so requite the Lord?

We cannot: for when we look we find that in the line of the seed of the promise (that of the Gentile believers as well as that of the law),—in this line of the promised seed, have been found from age to age the mass of those who have been saved. God bestows his grace where he has given his covenant; where he has deposited his word; where his ordinances are observed; and where the voice of prayer and of faith ascends. Pagan lands bear not the fruits of Christendom. Those places in Christendom, where the oracles of God, the preaching of the word, and the ordinances are not, are not visited with showers of grace and blessed with a godly seed, like those places where the ordinances and the word are enjoyed. The fathers of an ungodly community hand down ungodliness and perdition to their children; and often upon their children's children to the fourth generation are the iniquities of the fathers visited; no less by the laws of nature, than by the providence, and according to the word of God. The true worshippers of God bequeath their sanctuaries, their Sabbaths, and their divine ordinances, to their posterity; who have been imbued with the principles of Divine truth, and trained up in the nurture and admonition of the Lord. There the grace of God showers down the influence of the Holy Spirit. From these are taken those who are to be the sons and daughters of the Lord Almighty.

Shall we be told that all this is *natural*, and pertains not to the provision of the covenant? WHO MADE IT NATURAL? Do not the arrangements which God has made in the natural world show as well as any other, what is his pleasure? And do not they show us here that it is his pleasure to be the God of believers, and of their seed after them? Shall it be thought wonderful that he has ratified by covenant what he has appointed in nature? And if the covenant were to pass away, would not the great truth still remain true in nature, that God is pleased to be the God of believers, and of their seed after them?

But, *is it all natural?* Is there NO GRACE, in determining who shall be the heirs of salvation? Shall we be told that the covenant is nothing, because God has arranged powerful means to secure the fulfilment of his promises? Surely none can make this objection, who do not at the same time forget, that the grace of God which brings renewing and salvation to an individual soul, is quite beyond the effect of the most powerful means, and depends upon the sovereign act of a sovereign God. In giving his Spirit, he is sovereign; and his sovereignty works in such a way as to fulfil the promise of his covenant.

But when we look at this point more fully, the light breaks upon us in increasing splendor. An attention to facts shows that God does remember his covenant, and put honor upon its seal. From the published and official returns of the Congregational Churches of Connecticut to the General Association in 1834, it appears that two-thirds of all that were received to these Churches on profession of faith, the preceding year, had been baptized in infancy. Struck with this fact, I was curious to add up the results for several years, and found them very nearly the same. The results of an examination of like reports of Massachusetts, New Hampshire, and of the General Association of New York, were not essentially different. About two-thirds of all those received to our Pedobaptist Churches on confession of faith, are such as were baptized in their infancy.

But taking the whole field, the baptized children constitute, probably, not more than one-third of the children attached to the congregations of those churches, or falling properly to no other denomination. The state of the case, then, is this: out of *one*-third of a given population, *two* are hopefully converted, and brought into the Church, where there is *one* so converted out of the remaining *two*-thirds; a ratio of *four* to *one!* What will this amount to in the whole country? What in the whole world? What will it amount to if you trace it down to the end of time? To a "multitude which is as the sand by the sea-shore, innumerable!"

But in the Western and Southern parts of the country, the difference is more striking than in New England; because the proportion of the members of the Church of Christ to the whole population is far less. And these results are witnessed, when so much confident denunciation of Infant Baptism has led so many members of the church to neglect it; and led so many more to regard it as a mere ritual, rather than as the valuable seal of God's covenant. Oh, what might have been done, had parents taken hold of that covenant with unwavering faith; and, pleading the covenant, had taken encouragement from its promises, and from God's faithfulness, to be more earnest in the discharge of the duties which that covenant implies on the part of parents! Who is to answer for all this loss and harm? Who is to be responsible for teaching the Church of God to neglect and despise both the covenant and its seal?

But it is alleged that the children of Baptist families are blessed also. We are glad to believe it. We praise God for it. This proves that God is faithful to his covenant, even when his people have not the grace to own it, and give God thanks for it. It is the promise of the covenant that continues to them a godly seed. Is it not strange, while the fruit remains, that the tree should be accounted dead? But are they sure that the blessing follows in an equal degree that it would, did they acknowledge and plead the covenant? Are all these rich promises, these numerous and ample declarations, by which God engages to be the God of his people, and of their seed after them, so poor as to be thrown lightly away; and that for the strange reason that God has arranged the means of fulfilling them, and does actually fulfil them?

If our brethren choose to reject the covenant and its seal, will they not at least allow us and our children to enjoy it in peace? We have studied the matter as well as they. We have a conscience to answer as well as they. We have the Bible in our hands, and we know fully all the objections of our brethren. May we never enjoy in peace the ordinances which we truly hold dear, as granted us and enjoined upon us by the oracles of God? Are we never to have done hearing it ridiculed as "Popery," "superstition," and "mockery?" Is no respect due to our understanding?—none to our regard for the truth?—none to our religious integrity, and to our fear of God? And yet, what we are often compelled to hear, and what is often and diligently thrown upon the members of our churches, to deter them from this holy ordinance, take the following from a Baptist periodical as a specimen.

"If a parent is tempted to sprinkle his babe, he should remember, 1st. That he has no right to take advantage of the helpless state of his babe, and enslave it to usurpers; 2d. He has no right to countenance a mockery of Christ's ordinances; 3d. He has no right to dedicate his child in connection with a delusion; it will make him feel as if the matter were done up for life; 4th. He has no right to countenance a deluded and crazed minister solemnly telling a falsehood, however honest he may be in it, by saying, 'I baptize thee,' when he does no such thing; and by saying he does it in the name of the Trinity, when it is not so; 5th. There are so many false principles in the transaction, he should stop and consider well; he that doubteth is condemned if he do it. There is every reason to believe it to be a deception."

Fathers and mothers in the Church of God; have you ever felt, when you have claimed the privileges of the covenant for your children, that the mere application of the seal changed the hearts of these children or ensured that it would ever be done? Have you ever felt that, having done this, the matter was "done up for life?" Were you so instructed in your childhood? Did you ever feel so? Fathers and mothers in *this* Church of God:* ye whose memories embrace the days of Benedict, Eaton, Swan and Burnet: have you ever heard such a doctrine taught from this pulpit? Has anything that could countenance such a notion ever fallen upon your ears in this house of God? I look around and see many youths from whom it is not many months since I heard the inquiry, What shall we do to be saved? Dear youths, did it ever enter into your minds, that because you had been baptized, the business was done up for life; or that you were relieved at all from the necessity of being born of the spirit; of repenting and turning to God, if you would be saved?

I, too, am a parent. I know the hallowed and deep impressions of a parent in presenting his child to receive the seal of God's covenant; I know how strong is the impression made upon a parent's soul, that his offspring are the degenerate plants of a strange vine; fallen, depraved beings, who must receive the inward washing of regeneration, of which the outward baptism is but the sign, or be lost. I know it comforts a parent's heart, as he looks for-

---

* The First Church in Norwalk, Conn.

ward to the future life of that child, and forward to the eternal world; to be able to claim that blessed promise, "I will be thy God, and the God of thy seed after thee." I know how solemn is the impression made upon the parent's heart, of the covenant, which, in this transaction, he takes upon his soul, to train up his child in the nurture and admonition of the Lord.

It is vain for the world to inquire of the Christian, "What is the use of taking a morsel of bread and a little wine at the communion? Is there any benefit in a mere ceremony?" When the Christian has felt the presence of the Saviour at his table; when his soul has been kindled into a near communion with Christ, as the simple emblems of his Saviour's body and blood have set forth that Saviour's love, and sufferings, and faithfulness in connection with the tenderness of that dying charge —"*This do in remembrance of me.*" Oh, it is vain then for the world to ask him, What profit is there in a mere ceremony? So with the parent who has felt the influence of that solemn act — the baptism of his child—upon his own heart: and when, in after days, he *feels* how it encourages his faith, and deepens his sense of responsibility. Vain is all the language of reproach and ridicule then. Men may deride this faith, as well as reason against it. What then? Is there an article of his faith which has not been impugned and derided; and that too by men bearing the Christian name? The divinity of his Saviour is denied; the atonement is denied; the renewing of the Holy Ghost, and even his personal existence is denied. The inspiration of the Bible is denied; and now even the personal existence of the Godhead is denied; and all these things by men who call themselves by the name of Christ! If he is to yield every truth which is assailed, and abandon every point that is vehemently impugned and ridiculed, what has he left? His faith, his hope, his consolation, his Redeemer, his Sanctifier, his God, are gone.

"Prove all things: hold fast that which is good." This ground we have proved. We have listened to objections, we have weighed arguments. These have not moved us; how much less shall railing and reproaches move us from that which we have received to hold, as nothing less than an ordinance of the Most High God?

Let us believe. Let us obey. Let us not only be scrupulous to give our children the seal; but to teach them afterwards its import; to warn them how they slight its obligation, or undervalue its privileges. Let us make it the basis of our plea with our children, that they will not forsake the God of their fathers. Let us make it the ground of our plea with God, that he will give to our children the blessings of the covenant which are implied in the seal. Let us ask these things of our covenant keeping and faithful God. Let our souls never cease from the throes of earnest desire, till Christ be formed in our children, the hope of glory. Then, when households meet around the throne of God, may the parents and the children rejoice together with exceeding joy; and to the covenant mercy of God shall redound eternal praise.

Are there believing parents who have been misled concerning the truth; or who, through the want of a proper understanding of the ordinance; or through unbelief concerning its utility, have neglected to claim its blessings, and to affix the seal of the covenant upon their children? Have they now seen and understood the truth? Then seize the privileges of the covenant, and claim the seal for your children, if it yet remains within your power, and pray God not to visit your past unbelief or negligence upon you or upon your offspring. Cast not away the privileges of that gracious covenant, which the Lord has deemed worthy of HIM to offer to his children as a precious boon from their Father and their God.

Let those who are parents, and not yet savingly interested in the covenant of grace, feel for their children as well as for themselves. Perhaps, the seal of the covenant was given to you. "Perhaps, to you it descended from generation to generation, through an unbroken line of pious ancestry." It was a token that God, the God of your fathers, was ready to be your God and the God of your children, if you would not, by your own unbelief and guilt, cast away the blessings of the covenant. Shall the line be broken in you? Think how many generations of the descendants of them who disowned the Messiah, and were broken off and rejected from being the people of God, have wandered away, and stumbled and perished on the dark mountains. *Shall your children*, and perhaps your children's children, be thrown aside among the branches that are broken off?

It is true, that no one of them will perish, but for his own sin. But how many a child, and how many children's children do perish through the occasion and influence of an unbelieving and wicked father? I need only refer you to the influence of a Sabbath-breaker, an infidel, a scoffer, a profane, or lewd, or unprincipled man, upon the destinies of his children and more remote descendants. Can we be sure that there may be nothing like this in the influence of him who is the occasion of breaking away from the covenant and its seal, and of cutting his posterity off from privileges and means of grace which the piety of his ancestors, from generation to generation, handed down to him? Is there no such natural tendency or influence in the example of his unbelief? — none in his neglect of household prayer? — none in the separation of him and all his, from the sacraments of the Church of God? Remember and fear that solemn admonition of God to his covenant people of old — "Because thou hast rejected knowledge, I will also reject thee — seeing thou hast forgotten the law of thy God, I *will also forget thy children.*"

The branch may be broken off, but it is not for man to tell when it may, if ever, please God to graft it in again. Oh! son — daughter — of the covenant! what consequences — aside from the condemnation and ruin of your own soul — may arise from your unbelief, and descend in fruits of woe to generations that are yet unborn! Let the seal of the covenant, which was impressed upon you with the tender yearnings of parental faith, remind you of the blessings that you cast away in remaining alienated from God. Call not down upon your own head this double ruin. Break not away from the cords with which God himself would draw you to salvation. Defeat not the prayers of a father's faith and of a mother's love. Compel not the mercy, that waits to save you, to depart, and to give you up to the hand of justice, as one who, from the gates of heaven, *would* thrust himself down to the despair of hell.

CHILDREN of the COVENANT! ye who were in your infancy dedicated to God! Your parents by their acts bind you in secular matters. God and the laws of society have given them this prerogative, not for their advantage, but for yours. It is then no unprecedented thing, when you are by your parents given up to God and sealed with his seal. *He claims this right in you;* the neglect of your parents would not have altered his claim. But would you — if you could — that when God had graciously given his covenant for their advantage and for yours, that they had thrown away the covenant and denied you the seal? Choose you, then, to throw away proffered blessings, and having thrown them away, to take your lot with the world, with no portion but in the uncovenanted mercies of God?

Had a rich friend, in your infancy, offered to leave you an estate, if your parent would in your behalf undertake the trust and execute the forms, would you that your parent had refused the gift; and especially if the condition of the gift had obliged him carefully to train you up in the nurture and admonition of the Lord? Surely you would not be so unwise. Is the case altered when God himself is the giver, and proffers a richer portion than all the kingdoms of this world? Is God a foe to offer this covenant? Is your parent a foe to take and seal it? That seal is to you a token no less of privilege than of obligation. Will you throw these promises of God away? Will you determine to renounce your baptism, and render it null? You may, but not with ordinary guilt; especially if from infancy you have been the child of prayers and tears to God for your salvation. Oh! how rich this boon of the covenant and its seal, which thus pleads with you, our children, to be the children of your father's God! Will you disavow the covenant and the seal? Will you disown the obligation which they impose on you to love and serve Jehovah, your father's covenant God? You may be so infatuated, but God will not for this release you from the obligation. You may sell your birthright like Esau, but, like Esau, you may find no place for repentance, though you seek it carefully with tears.

O, God of our fathers! our covenant God! Save our children from such a doom as this! Seal them thine own, by working in their souls the reality of that which is signified by the outward sign. Make them thine own by the washing of regeneration and the renewing of the Holy Ghost, and thy name shall have all the praise, for ever. Amen.

THE END.

www.ingramcontent.com/pod-product-compliance
Lightning Source LLC
Chambersburg PA
CBHW031812230426
43669CB00009B/1106